CW01650645

Healthy noodles

Healthy noodles

fresh ideas for all sorts of noodles

kurumi hayter

TED SMART

A QUINTET BOOK

This edition produced for
The Book People Ltd
Hall Wood Avenue
Haydock
St Helens WA11 9UL

Copyright © 1999 Quintet Publishing Limited.
All rights reserved. No part of this publication may be reproduced, stored in a retrieval system or transmitted in any form or by any means, electronic, mechanical, photocopying, recording or otherwise, without the permission of the copyright holder.

ISBN 1-85613-731-7

This book was designed and produced by
Quintet Publishing Limited
6 Blundell Street
London N7 9BH

Creative Director: **Richard Dewing**
Art Director: **Paula Marchant**
Designer: **Jacqui Ellis-Dodds**
Project Editor: **Amanda Dixon**
Editor: **Lyn Coutts**
Photographers: **David Armstrong, Howard Shooter, Ian Garlick, and Tim Ferguson-Hill**
Food Stylist: **Kurumi Hayter**

Picture Credits
Life File: pages 6(t), (b), 7(t), 9(t).
Axiom Photographic Agency: pages 7(b), 8(t), 9(b)
A Dixon: page 8(b)

Material in this book has previously appeared in *Japanese Cooking for Two* by Kurumi Hayter, *Korean Cooking* by Hilaire Walden, *The Noodle Cookbook* by Kurumi Hayter, *Stir Fry Cooking* by Bridget Jones, and *Vietnamese Cooking* by Paulette Do Van.

Typeset in Great Britain by Central Southern Typesetters, Eastbourne
Manufactured in Hong Kong by Regent Publishing Services Ltd.
Printed in Singapore by Star Standard Industries Pte Ltd.

contents

noodles nood

Noodles are the 'fast food' of Oriental cuisine in the same way as pasta is a staple in Italian cooking. Some food historians even go so far as to claim that noodles were the first convenience food, and that they are the fastest fast food. But while most Western store cupboards contain packets of pasta so that a nutritious and tasty meal can be rustled up in a few minutes, in very few will you find a stock of dried noodles. But why should this be the case when noodles really are the perfect food?

▲ Morning market in Mandalay, Myanmar (Burma).

You will find noodles served from a roadside stall in the desolate wastes of northern China, in bustling restaurants in the heart of the Tokyo's financial district, and on the beaches of Thailand and Indonesia. Throughout Southeast Asia, the noodle is ubiquitous, and challenges rice as the main staple.

In dried or parboiled form, noodles have a generous shelf-life, are inexpensive, and very easy to prepare. Noodles are also healthy and nutritious, and they can complement any dish – even those that have never seen the inside of a Japanese, Korean, Chinese, Vietnamese, Thai, Malaysian or Indonesian kitchen, or rubbed shoulders with the flavoursome ingredients of these cuisines.

▼ Wheat fields, Yunnan Province, China.

noodles

Noodles are nothing if not versatile. They can be made into a nourishing and filling meal accompanied by a broth or soup, or made into a nest filled with stir-fried meat, fish or vegetables for a hearty meal to warm the coldest night. They can be served in a salad, or over ice and topped with a sauce as a refreshing summer dish. And all the while, noodles are doing you a favour.

Noodles are high in carbohydrates, low in fat, and basically devoid of additives, flavour enhancers and colourings. In a usual serving, the proportion of noodles and vegetables is high in relation to animal products, so they are a very healthy dietary alternative. More so, if you follow the tradition of Southeast Asian cuisines by using fish rather than meat protein.

▲ Noodles drying, Yunnan Province, China.

The aim of this book is to get the noodle revolution happening in your kitchen. It will tell you everything you need to know about buying, storing and choosing noodles, and how to prepare them. Then, loaded with confidence and a store cupboard stacked high with noodles, you can work your way through the 66 recipes. The recipes are divided into four chapters, each chapter dealing with one type of noodle. The recipes vary in complexity – some are ready in minutes, others will take longer. But of one thing you can be certain – the actual noodles are always ready in minutes!

◀ Eating noodle soup in the street, Lanzhou, Gansu Province, China.

noodles nood

▲ Making and cooking traditional noodles, Kashgar, Xinjiang Province, China.

Choosing and Buying Noodles

There are almost 20 varieties of noodles available, and they are made from basic ingredients like egg, wheat, buckwheat, rice or mung bean flours and water. Each type of noodle requires different treatment. Some noodles are best stir-fried, while others are better boiled and served in a broth or soup. Details of how to cook and use noodles is given on pages 10 to 15.

Large supermarkets will stock a range of dried noodles, and some may have a selection of fresh and parboiled noodles. Specialist food shops will carry a wider selection, though nothing really beats a visit to a Japanese or Chinese food shop. Not only will the range be daunting and include hard-to-find varieties of fresh noodles, but the staff can offer expert advice and you can pick up any other ingredients you may need.

Once at home, fresh and steamed noodles should be stored in a refrigerator and consumed within two or three days. Most fresh noodles and some parboiled noodles can be frozen. Only fresh *udon* do not freeze well. Dried noodles have an extensive shelf life if stored in an airtight container. Parboiled noodles are usually sold in sealed packs, with storage instructions and 'use by' date clearly marked.

Serving Noodles

It is most important that noodles are freshly prepared. No elegant serving plate will compensate for noodles that are overcooked, dull (perfectly-cooked noodles have a sheen) and stuck together in a formless lump.

◀ Busy street in Kowloon, Hong Kong.

Paddy fields, Lombok, Indonesia.

A noodle dish looks most appetizing when served on a large plate or in a large shallow bowl if the recipe has a lot of sauce. Noodle soups are served in individual, deep bowls.

About the Recipes in This Book

All recipes serve four, unless otherwise stated at the beginning of the recipe. The soaking and cooking times for noodles are approximate, as they will vary from brand to brand. Always check the instructions on the packet.

Eating noodles, Japan.

noodles nood

▲ thin egg noodles, dried

▲ medium egg noodles, dried

▲ Japanese *ramen* noodles, fresh

▲ Japanese steamed egg noodles, fresh

EGG NOODLES

Egg noodles are made from eggs and wheat flour, and are eaten widely throughout Southeast Asia both in soups and in stir-fry dishes. The types of egg noodles used in the recipes are: thin egg noodles, medium egg noodles, Japanese fresh *ramen* and Japanese steamed egg noodles.

Thin and medium egg noodles can be bought dried or fresh. In their dried form, the noodles are often compressed into blocks. Once dropped into boiling water, the tangled mass of noodles unravels in separate stands. Thin egg noodles are also known as thread egg noodles. Whether fresh or dried, egg noodles are ideal for stir-fry dishes. Once boiled and drained, they can also be deep-fried to make crispy noodles.

Japanese *ramen* and steamed egg noodles are available fresh, often lightly compacted in sealed bags. Some come packaged with a ready-made soup or sauce. The texture of the fresh noodles makes them best for use in hot noodle soups, though Japanese steamed noodles are put to good use in stir-fry dishes.

cooking times

Thin egg noodles, fresh or dried
boil for 3 minutes.

Medium egg noodles, fresh or dried
boil for 3 to 4 minutes.

Japanese *ramen* noodles, fresh
boil for 2 to 3 minutes.

Japanese steamed egg noodles, fresh
rinse in boiling water.

RICE NOODLES

Rice noodles are made from rice flour and water, and are available fresh or dried in three thicknesses – very fine, tagliatelle-size and wide. Rice noodles are used in soups and stir-fries, and can be deep-fried for crispy noodles. Rice noodles are soaked in warm or hot water, not cooked, prior to being added to a dish.

▲ rice vermicelli, dried

Rice vermicelli are very fine noodles, most usually available in dried form. This cream-coloured noodle is sold in bundles that resemble a mass of 'angel's hair.' Rice vermicelli can be served 'soft', stir-fried or deep-fried. To deep-fry, the dried noodles are placed directly into hot oil.

▲ rice stick noodles, dried

Rice stick noodles are made from rice flour, starch and water, and resemble Italian tagliatelle. Though always flat, different widths and thicknesses of rice stick noodles are available.

Steamed flat rice noodles are about one centimetre/half an inch in width, and they are usually sold fresh in compressed blocks. The Chinese know them as *ho fun*, the Thai as *sen men*, and the Vietnamese as *banh pho*.

▲ steamed flat rice noodles, fresh

cooking times

Rice vermicelli, dried
3 to 5 minutes in warm water.

Rice stick noodles, dried
2 to 5 minutes in warm water.

Steamed flat rice noodles, fresh
rinse in hot water.

noodles nood

▲ *udon*, freshly made

▲ *udon*, parboiled

▲ flat *kishimen udon*, dried

▲ round *udon*, dried

WHEAT NOODLES – *UDON, SOBA* AND *SOMEN*

Once found only in Japanese, Korean, and Chinese grocers or specialist food shops, *udon*, *soba* and *somen* can now be found on many supermarket shelves. While *udon* seems to be the most easily available, it will not be long before *soba* and *somen* are given equal shelf space.

Udon are made from wheat flour and water, and come in many forms – thin to thick, flat or round and dried or parboiled. At a Japanese food shop you may even be able to buy freshly made *udon*. Flat ribbons of *udon* are known as *kishimen*. Use *udon* in hot noodle soups, cold dishes and stir-fries.

Soba have a distinctive flavour resulting from being made from buckwheat and wheat flour. The buckwheat also gives them a distinctive brown colour. They are highly nutritious and rich in protein and lecithin. Japanese and Chinese shops sell dried, fresh and parboiled *soba*, though hot dried *soba* is the easiest to find. Korean buckwheat noodles are called *son myon*. *Soba* noodles can be served cold or in hot soups.

Somen are made from wheat flour and water and are only sold in dried form, which should be handled carefully as they are very fragile. *Somen*, which resemble spaghetti pasta, are commonly used for cold summer dishes, but can also be used in hot noodle soups.

noodles

cooking times

***Udon*, freshly made**
boil for 13 to 15 minutes.

***Udon*, parboiled**
boil for 3 minutes.

Flat *kishimen udon*, dried
boil for 3 to 4 minutes.

Round *udon*, dried
boil for 7 to 15 minutes depending on thickness.

***Soba*, dried**
boil for 5 to 6 minutes.

***Somen*, dried**
boil for 1 to 2 minutes.

▲ *soba*, dried

▲ *somen*, dried

▲ bean thread vermicelli, dried

BEAN THREAD NOODLES

Bean thread noodles are made from the dried and strained liquid of puréed green mung beans, and resemble strands of clear plastic. Because of this, these dried noodles are also known as cellophane, glass or transparent noodles. The fineness of the noodles has earned them the tag 'vermicelli', though they are in fact tougher than rice vermicelli. This toughness means that bundles of bean thread noodles need to be soaked prior to being added to a dish. Once soaked, the noodles become soft, slippery and gelatinous. Bean thread noodles are used in soups, braised dishes, stir-fries and hotpots.

cooking times

Bean thread vermicelli, dried
boil for 5 minutes

noodles nood

HOW TO COOK NOODLES

Cooking noodles is simplicity itself. All that is needed is a wok or large pan and water. The most essential thing about noodles is cooking until the texture is just right – *al dente* like Italian pasta. Noodles absorb water – and any other liquid – very rapidly and nothing ruins them like overcooking.

Noodles are prepared by being boiled, soaked or rinsed in water.

Egg noodles and *Ramen* – bring a large quantity of water to the boil in a wok or pan, then add the noodles. Stir a couple of times to prevent the noodles from sticking together.

Rice noodles – fill a large bowl or pan with warm water and add the noodles. The soaking time depends on their thickness, so check the instructions on the packet. When ready, rinse under cold water and drain.

Udon* and *Soba – bring a large quantity of water to the boil in a pan, add the noodles and stir a couple of times. When the water returns to the boil, pour in a small cupful of cold water to lower the temperature. When the water comes back to the boil, add more cold water. The boiling time depends on whether *udon* or *soba* is used, and on the thickness of the noodles themselves. Rinse well under cold water and drain.

Somen – bring a large quantity of water to the boil in a pan, immerse the noodles and stir a couple of times. When the water returns to the boil, add a small cupful of cold water. Remove the noodles when the water returns to a rolling boil. Rinse well under cold water and drain.

Bean thread noodles – add the bean thread noodles to a large bowl or pan filled with boiling water. Soak for the period stated on the packet, then rinse under cold water and drain.

▶ boiling egg noodles

AFTER COOKING AND SOAKING

The noodles are the last thing to be cooked – everything else for the meal should be ready. If the noodles are being used in a hot noodle soup, for example, pour over the broth just before you are going to eat. Noodles tend to stick together if left for even a short time after cooking.

UTENSILS

Wok – though a large pan or frying pan can replace a wok, there is nothing like having the real thing. A wok is versatile; one moment it's boiling, soaking or steaming, the next stir-frying, deep-frying or braising. And it does it all quickly and in an energy efficient way, and in the case of frying, with the minimum amount of oil.

After use, a wok should be scrubbed with a brush in hot water – no detergents! Hand dry, then place the wok over a low heat for one minute to evaporate any moisture and therefore prevent rusting. Before storing, rub the inside of the wok with a little oil. The only time detergent should come into contact with a wok is if rust has formed.

Sieve – this is vital for draining noodles rapidly once they are cooked. Sieves can be made of metal or plastic, or there is the more authentic bamboo version with its metal net.

Slotted spoon – a non-essential item, but one that can come in handy for moving food around a wok (cooked foods are often pushed to the side of the wok to allow something else to be cooked in the middle) and for selectively removing ingredients while others continue cooking.

▶ Two designs of wok, one with the traditional long wooden handle and the other with two carrying handles. The brush may be used to oil woks, and the strainers are useful accessories for some recipes.

INGREDIENTS

Many of the ingredients listed here can be bought from your local supermarket or grocery shop. The rest can be found in Japanese or other Oriental food shops. Health shops also commonly stock a number of the more unusual ingredients.

▲ bamboo shoots

Bamboo shoots – parboiled or tinned bamboo shoots are widely available. Cooked dried bamboo shoots (*shinachiku*) are also available.

Banh trang – semi-transparent hard rice-paper from Vietnam used for wrapping spring rolls and grilled meats. Before use, moisten and dip *banh trang* in warm water.

▲ bean curd (*tofu*)

Bean curd – also known as tofu or 'meat without bones', bean curd is high in protein and low in fat. It is bought in soft blocks and absorbs the flavour of other ingredients. Deep-fried bean curd (*abura-age*) is bought ready-made in sheets from specialist groceries. Before use, rinse with hot water to remove excess oil.

▲ bonito flakes (*katsuo-bushi*)

Bean sprouts – crunchy and tender germinated sprouts of the mung bean, commonly used in Chinese cooking. Eaten raw or very lightly stir-fried, bean sprouts can be kept refrigerated in plastic bags for up to 3 days. Avoid tinned bean sprouts which lack flavour and texture.

Black bean sauce – made from black beans that have been salted, then fermented with a variety of spices widely used in Southeast Asian cooking.

Bonito flakes (*katsuo-bushi*) – essential ingredient of Japanese cuisine, mainly used in making stock. Available in blocks or more commonly, ready-flaked. Store in the refrigerator.

▲ chilli oil

Chilli oil – red-coloured oil made from ground chillies. Indonesian chilli sauce (*sambal oelek*) is a paste made from crushed red chillies.

Chinese barbecued pork *(cha siu)* – made by marinating 500 g/1 lb pork tenderloin in 4 tablespoons *cha siu* sauce for 3 to 4 hours. Place on a rack on a baking tray lined with foil in an oven pre-heated to 375°F/190°C/Gas mark 5. Bake for 60 to 70 minutes, basting a few times. The outside of the pork should be browned and the inside still tender.

Coconut milk – squeezed from the flesh of the coconut, coconut milk is available tinned or powdered. It is high in saturated fats.

Dried kelp *(konbu)* – dark brown to greyish-black in colour, kelp is essential for Japanese stocks. Wipe with a damp cloth before use.

Dried prawns – salty, hard, whole prawns used to add flavour. Malaysian dried shrimp paste (*belacan*) has a strong smell and must be fried before use.

Fermented soybeans (*natto*) – sticky sauce with a distinctive odour, high in fibre and protein.

Fish sauce (*shottsuru, nam pla, nuoc nam* or *patis*) light brown, thin sauce made from salted, fermented fish. Though its smell and taste are distinctive, soy sauce can be substituted.

Five-spice powder – aromatic Chinese spice that can be bought prepared or made by grinding 40 Szechwan peppercorns, two 5-centimetre/2-inch cinnamon sticks, 1½ teaspoons fennel seeds, 12 cloves and 2 star anise in a mortar and pestle to a fine powder.

Green seaweed *(wakame)* – green seaweed pieces that are thinner than kelp. Bought fresh, salted or dried. Dried *wakame* has to be soaked before use.

Japanese horseradish *(wasabi)* – also known as Japanese green mustard, this is the grated root of a riverside plant native to Japan. Fresh *wasabi* is expensive, so a paste or powder is used instead.

Kaffir lime leaves *(bai makrat)* – widely used in Thai cooking, they are sold fresh or dried.

Lemon grass – also known as citronella, it has a distinct lemon scent and flavour.

***Miso* paste** – made from fermented cooked soy beans, this salty, soy bean product comes in a

▲ dried kelp *(konbu)*

▲ dried shrimps

▲ fermented soy beans *(natto)*

▲ green seaweed *(wakame)*

▲ Japanese horseradish *(wasabi)*

▲ lemon grass

▲ *miso* paste

▲ *nameko* mushrooms

variety of flavours, colours and textures. Red *miso* has a stronger flavour than white *miso*. It is highly nutritious, easy to digest, and low-salt varieties are available. Store in the refrigerator.

***Nameko* mushrooms** – small Japanese mushrooms with a light brown cap and slippery outer coating. They are also available tinned. Tinned button mushrooms can be substituted.

Oyster sauce – thick, rich sauce made from extract of oysters and salt and soy sauce.

Pickled ginger (*gari*) – cream or pink paper-thin slices of ginger pickled with sugar and vinegar, used as a garnish in Japanese dishes.

Red curry paste – sometimes known as Thai curry paste, it has a hot, sour taste. It is a combination of chillies, lemon grass, spring onions, ginger, dried shrimp paste, coriander, fennel and other spices.

Red pickled ginger (*beni-shoga*) – red shreds of ginger, pickled with sugar and vinegar, with a hotter taste than pickled ginger.

Rice wine – made from fermented freshly steamed short-grain rice, water and an enzyme. Japanese varieties include crystal-clear *sake* and *mirin* (*see* sweet rice wine). Chinese varieties of rice wine include Chia Fan, Hsiang Hsueh, Shan Niang and Yen Hung brands.

Seaweed paper *(nori)* – laver seaweed that has been dried into paper-thin sheets. It is lightly toasted before use or can be bought pre-toasted (labelled *yakinori*).

Sesame paste – this thick paste, creamy-white in colour, is made from ground sesame seeds.

Sesame seeds – can be used as are, but toasting brings out their nutty aroma. To toast, heat a heavy frying pan and then add the sesame seeds. Do not add any oil. Stir or shake the pan until the seeds swell up and darken slightly.

Seven-spice seasoning *(shichimi togarashi)* – grainy Japanese mixture of red chilli pepper, Chinese pepper, dried orange peel, sesame seeds, poppy seeds, slivers of *nori* seaweed paper and hemp seeds; the exact blend of slices varies.

***Shiitake* mushrooms** – can be bought fresh or dried, they have a smoky smell. Soak dried mushrooms in warm water for 20 minutes and remove the stalks before using.

Shrimp paste – made from ground salted, fermented shrimps, is sold as a pink-coloured paste or in brown-coloured cakes.

Soured plums *(ume-boshi)* – traditional Japanese preserved food made from green plums.

Soy sauce – Chinese soy sauce (*jiang yong*) and Japanese soy sauce (*shoyu*) are both widely available although very different in taste. Always try to use the type specified in the recipe. Chinese light soy sauce is salty and used as a flavouring, and Chinese dark soy sauce is less salty with a fuller flavour and a hint of sweetness. Japanese soy sauce is lighter than the Chinese varieties, has wheat added to it, and has a sweeter taste.

Star anise – native to China, this tan-coloured, eight-pointed seed pod has a liquorice flavour.

Straw mushrooms – small oval-shaped mushrooms with dark brown caps, commonly used in Chinese cooking. They are available tinned.

Sweet rice wine *(mirin)* – used as a sweetener in cooking, with a low alcohol content and not for drinking.

Tamarind juice – a sour, dark liquid strained from dried tamarind fruit.

White radish *(daikon)* – also known as *mooli*, it can be eaten raw or cooked. It is also used for decorative garnishes. It is said to be calorie-free and to be good for the digestion.

Wood ear fungus – valued for its subtle flavour and slightly crunchy 'bite', this mushroom is sold dried and resembles curly seaweed. It is soaked for 20 to 30 minutes before use and expands to five times its dried size.

▲ pickled ginger *(gari)*

▲ seaweed paper *(nori)*

▲ seven-spice seasoning *(shichimi)*

▲ white radish *(daikon)*

cutting te

CUTTING TECHNIQUES

'Chopstick cultures' demand that most food be chopped or sliced into bite-sized pieces before cooking, so a well-sharpened knife is essential. As the origins of the noodle stem from Chinese cuisine, most noodle-based dishes follow this basic precept even though the fork and spoon are used in place of chopsticks in countries such as Thailand and Indonesia.

Mincing

Cut meat or vegetables into thin slices, then chop very finely.

Dicing

Cut vegetables, meat or bean curd into cubes roughly two centimetres/three quarters of an inch square.

Random cutting

Cut and roll vegetables at the same time to produce differently shaped pieces. Each piece should be roughly the same size.

Diagonal slicing
Cut on the diagonal to create more interesting slices and to increase the surface of the slice in preparation for cutting matchsticks or shredding.

Shredding
Cut the vegetable into very thin slices, then cut the slices very finely. If the vegetable is sliced on the diagonal, the shreds will curl to form a decorative garnish.

Matchsticks
Cut the vegetable into slices, then cut each slice into thin sticks. To get long matchsticks, slice cucumbers, white radish and carrots on the diagonal.

Slanted cutting
Half freeze the meat, then cut, slanting the knife in the direction of the cut to get the thinnest slices.

broths stocks

STOCKS AND BROTHS

If you have no time to prepare your own stock, instant stocks are available from specialist food shops. Vegetable Stock (see page 23) can be used instead of Chicken Stock in the recipes. You can keep fresh stocks and broths in the refrigerator for a few days or freeze them for later use.

Miso Broth (used for *ramen*)

Makes 1.4 L/2½ pt

1 Tbsp sesame oil
1 centimetre/½ inch piece root ginger, peeled and crushed
1 clove garlic, crushed
1 spring onion, finely chopped and crushed
4 Tbsp rice wine
3 Tbsp Japanese soy sauce or Chinese light soy sauce
2 Tbsp caster sugar
8 Tbsp red miso paste
2 tsp chilli oil
1.4 L/2½ pt Chicken Stock (see page 22)
Freshly ground black pepper

Heat the oil in a pan, and fry the ginger, garlic and spring onion for 30 seconds. Add the wine, then the soy sauce, sugar, *miso* paste and chilli oil, and mix together. Pour in the stock and bring to the boil. Remove from the heat. The broth is now ready for use.

Chicken Stock

Makes 1.8 L/3¼ pt

600 g/1¼ lb chicken bones, washed and roughly chopped
125 g/4 oz pork bones, washed
1 small onion, halved
1 leek, halved diagonally
2 cloves garlic, crushed
2.5-centimetre/1 inch piece root ginger, peeled and sliced
2 L/3½ pt water

Blanch the chicken and pork bones in boiling water for 2 minutes, then rinse. Put the bones and remaining ingredients in a large pan. Bring to the boil, then simmer for 1 hour, skimming off the scum occasionally. Strain the stock through a fine mesh sieve or muslin ready for use.

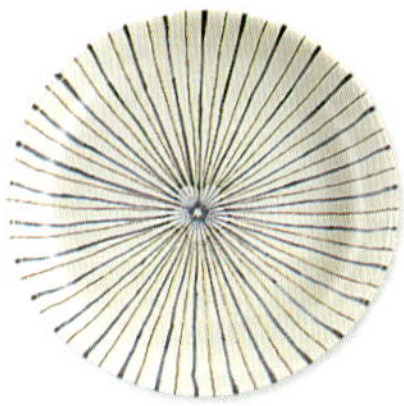

stocks broths

Light Chicken Stock

Makes 1.4 L/2½ pt

1.6 L/2¾ pt water

3 chicken drumsticks

Put the water and chicken drumsticks in a pan, and bring to the boil then simmer for 40 minutes or until the meat begins to fall away from the bone. Strain through a fine mesh sieve or muslin ready for use.

Soy Sauce Broth (used for *ramen*)

Makes 1.4 L/2½ pt

1.4 L/2½ pt Chicken Stock (see page 22)

2 tsp salt

4 tsp rice wine

4 Tbsp Japanese soy sauce or Chinese light soy sauce

4 tsp Chinese dark soy sauce

Freshly ground black pepper

Put the stock, salt and rice wine in a pan and bring to the boil, then simmer for 2 to 3 minutes. Turn off the heat and stir in the remaining ingredients. The broth is now ready for use.

Vegetable Stock

Makes 900 ml/1½ pt

1 Tbsp vegetable oil

1 clove garlic, sliced

2.5-centimetre/1-inch piece root ginger, peeled and sliced

1 leek, sliced

1 carrot, sliced

1 medium onion, chopped

1½ sticks celery, chopped

1.1 L/2 pt water

Heat the oil in a pan and fry all the vegetables for 2 minutes. Pour in the water and bring to the boil, then simmer for 40 minutes. Strain through a fine mesh sieve or muslin ready for use.

Premier Japanese Stock (*Dashi*)

Makes 1.4 L/2½ pt

1.4 L/2½ pt water

10 centimetres/4 inches dried kelp, wiped with a damp cloth

50 g/2 oz bonito flakes

Make two or three cuts about 2.5 centimetres/l-inch long in the dried kelp to release more flavour. Put the dried kelp and water into a pan and heat gently. Remove the dried kelp just before the water begins to boil. Add the bonito flakes when the water boils and turn off the heat. When the flakes sink to the bottom, strain the stock through a paper filter or muslin ready for use.

broths stocks

▲ ingredients for Vegetable Stock

Japanese Broth (used for *udon*, *soba* and *somen* noodles)

Makes 1.4 L/2½ pt

2 Tbsp sweet rice wine
1.4 L/2½ pt Premier Japanese Stock (see page 23)
5 Tbsp light or Japanese soy sauce
3 Tbsp caster sugar

Put the sweet rice wine in a pan and bring to the boil. Add the remaining ingredients and simmer for 3 to 4 minutes. The broth is ready for use.

Dipping Broth

Makes 850 ml/1½ pt

150 ml/5 fl oz sweet rice wine
500 ml/1 pt Premier Japanese Stock (see page 23)
150 ml/5 fl oz Japanese soy sauce

Put the sweet rice wine in a pan and bring to the boil. Add the remaining ingredients and simmer for 3 to 4 minutes. Remove from the heat, leave the liquid to cool then chill in a sealed container in a refrigerator ready for use.

egg noodles

chapter 1

Vegetable and Noodle Stir-fry

The essence of a healthy meal – fresh, quality ingredients cooked simply and quickly. What could be better?

2 Tbsp vegetable oil
1 Tbsp sesame oil
1 small onion, sliced
75 g/3 oz mange tout, halved diagonally
1 small carrot, thinly sliced diagonally
200 g/7 oz bean sprouts
200 g/7 oz Chinese leaves, chopped
2 dried black wood ear fungi or dried *shiitaki* mushrooms, soaked in water, rinsed and chopped
Salt and pepper
500 g/1 lb ramen noodles, or 325 g/11 oz dried, thin egg noodles
1.4 L/2½ pt Soy Sauce Broth (see page 23)

▶ Heat the oils in a wok or frying pan until very hot. Stir-fry the onion, mange tout, and carrot for 2 minutes, add the bean sprouts, Chinese leaves and wood ear fungi and stir-fry for 4 minutes. Season with salt and pepper.

▶ Bring a large pan of water to the boil and add the noodles. Cook for 3 minutes before draining. Divide the noodles among four bowls.

▶ Heat the broth in a pan. Pile the vegetables onto the noodles and pour over the heated broth. Serve immediately.

Miso with Shredded Leek and Noodles

Always use a good-quality *miso* paste. Generally speaking, the more you pay for *miso* paste, the better quality it will be.

225 g/8 oz fresh spinach
450 g/1 lb *ramen* noodles, or 325 g/11 oz dried egg noodles
1.4 L/2½ pt *Miso* Broth (see page 22)
10-centimetre/4-inch piece leek, shredded
4 Tbsp cooked dried bamboo shoots (optional)

▶ Bring a little water to the boil in a pan and blanch the spinach for 1 to 2 minutes. Rinse, drain and set aside.

▶ Bring a large pan of water to the boil, add the noodles and boil for 4 minutes. Drain and divide among four bowls.

▶ Heat the *Miso* Broth for 2 to 3 minutes. Top the noodles with the leek, spinach and bamboo shoots. Pour on the broth and serve immediately.

Fish Balls with Crispy Vegetables and Noodles

If you are in a hurry, buy ready-made fish balls at a specialist shop.

fish balls

900 g/2 lb white fish, skinned and cut in chunks
3 Tbsp cornflour
1 egg white
Salt and freshly ground white pepper

noodles and vegetables

375 g/12 oz dried egg noodles
3 Tbsp oil
4 thin slices fresh root ginger
1 piece lemon grass or strip of lemon rind
1 stick celery, thinly sliced diagonally
1 bunch spring onions, sliced
125 g/4 oz mange tout, trimmed
3 Tbsp Chinese light soy sauce
3 Tbsp dry sherry

▶ Pound the fish with the cornstarch until it is reduced to a paste, then work in the egg white and seasoning. Wet your hands and shape the mixture into small balls. Boil the fish balls in a pan for 4 to 5 minutes, then drain.

▶ Place the noodles in a pan and pour over boiling water to cover. Bring back to the boil and cook for 2 minutes, then drain and set aside.

▶ Heat the oil in a wok or frying pan, then stir-fry the ginger and lemon grass for 1 minute before adding the fish balls. Stir-fry the fish balls until lightly browned. Add the celery, spring onions and mange tout and stir-fry until the vegetables are tender but crisp. Add the noodles, soy sauce and sherry. Stir the mixture over a high heat until the noodles are hot. Serve immediately.

Seaweed and Egg Noodle Soup

This is a classic Japanese soup. Seaweed is very nutritious, full of vitamins and minerals and virtually calorie-free. The dried varieties of seaweed are easily preserved and handled.

325 g/11 oz dried, medium egg noodles, or 450 g/1 lb *ramen* noodles
1.4 L/2½ pt Soy Sauce Broth (see page 23)
2½ Tbsp dried green seaweed, soaked in hot water and drained
4 Tbsp cooked, dried bamboo shoots (optional)
2 spring onions, chopped
2 hard-boiled eggs, halved

- Bring a large pan of water to the boil. Add the noodles and cook for 4 minutes. Drain and divide among four bowls.
- Heat the Soy Sauce Broth in a pan.
- Arrange the seaweed, bamboo shoots, spring onions and eggs on the noodles. Pour over the heated broth and serve immediately.

Malaysian Satay Noodles

The perfect vegetarian dish for those with a taste for piquant *satay* sauce.

2 Tbsp peanut oil
225 g/8 oz broccoli florets
1 carrot, cut into strips
1 leek, sliced
1 courgette, sliced
4 spring onions, sliced
1 green chilli, sliced
150 g/5 oz chunky peanut butter
5 Tbsp coconut milk
1 Tbsp lime juice
2 Tbsp Japanese soy sauce or Chinese light soy sauce
1 Tbsp chilli sauce
900 g/2 lb dried egg noodles

▶ Heat the oil in a wok or large frying pan and stir-fry the vegetables for 3 to 4 minutes. Meanwhile, put the peanut butter, coconut milk, lime juice, soy sauce and chilli sauce in a pan. Stir over a gentle heat until well mixed and hot.

▶ Place the noodles in a pan and pour over boiling water to cover. Cook for 3 minutes and drain. Pour over the peanut sauce and serve immediately.

Chinese-style Noodles with Wantons

Chinese *wantons* are parcels of minced meat, usually pork. Ground chicken can replace pork in this classic Chinese recipe. *Wanton* wrappers are available from specialist shops

Wanton filling
75 g/3 oz minced, lean pork or chicken, or vegetarian substitute
1 spring onion, finely chopped
1 dried *shiitake* mushroom, soaked in hot water, and very finely chopped
5-millimetre/¼-inch piece root ginger, peeled and sliced
½ tsp Chinese light soy sauce
¼ tsp sweet rice wine or dry sherry
¼ tsp sesame oil
Salt
20 *wanton* wrappers
325 g/11 oz fresh, thin egg noodles
1.4 L/2½ pt Soy Sauce Broth (see page 23)
2 large iceberg lettuce leaves, halved and blanched
3 spring onions, chopped

▶ Mix the ingredients for the *wanton* filling together in a bowl. Place 1 teaspoon of the filling in the middle of a *wanton* wrapper. Wet the edge with water and fold to form a clam shape. Press out air bubbles while sealing the edges. Draw up the two sides, wetting one with water, and pinch together. Repeat to use all the mixture.

▶ Bring two saucepans of water to the boil. Cook the noodles in one pan for 3 minutes. In the other, boil the *wantons* for about 3 to 4 minutes. Divide the noodles among four bowls, and top with *wantons*.

▶ Heat the broth. Arrange the lettuce and spring onions on the noodles and pour over the heated broth. Serve immediately.

Chilled Tuna and Prawn Noodle Salad

The topping on this dish is a modern and innovative use of easy-to-obtain ingredients. It is a refreshing, light meal that is perfect for a summer lunch or supper. Because noodles, even cold ones, dry out quickly, serve and devour this salad the moment it is ready.

450 g/1 lb fresh, thin egg noodles
2 tsp sesame oil

dressing

4 Tbsp sesame paste
4 Tbsp caster sugar
4 Tbsp vinegar
4 Tbsp Japanese soy sauce or Chinese light soy sauce
4 Tbsp Chicken Stock (see page 22)
1-centimetre/½-inch piece root ginger

topping

4 tsp dried green seaweed, soaked in hot water, then drained
200 g/7 oz tinned tuna in brine
8 Tbsp tinned sweetcorn
225 g/8 oz cooked prawns, shelled and deveined
Radish sprouts or watercress

▶ Bring a large pan of water to the boil and cook the noodles for 3 minutes. Rinse and drain, then toss in 2 teaspoons of sesame oil. Divide the noodles among four plates.

▶ Mix together the sesame paste, sugar, vinegar, soy sauce and stock. Chop the ginger very finely, then squeeze out the juice by hand. Add the juice to the mixture and stir in. Cover and chill in the refrigerator.

▶ Divide the topping ingredients among the four plates, and pour over the chilled dressing. Serve immediately.

Chinese Chicken and Peanut Sauce Noodle Salad

This very popular Chinese dish can be made with either smooth or chunky peanut butter. It is delicious with noodles.

450 g/1 lb boneless chicken breasts
450 g/1 lb fresh, thin egg noodles
2 tsp sesame oil
1 cucumber, thinly sliced diagonally, then cut into matchsticks

peanut sauce

8 Tbsp peanut butter
6 Tbsp caster sugar
4 Tbsp vinegar
5 Tbsp Chicken Stock (see page 22)
3 Tbsp Japanese soy sauce or Chinese light soy sauce
1 Tbsp Chinese dark soy sauce
1 tsp sesame oil
1 tsp chilli oil

▶ Put the chicken in a large pan of water and bring to the boil, then simmer for 20 minutes or until cooked. Occasionally skim the scum from the surface. Remove and allow to cool before removing the skin and tearing the chicken into bite-sized pieces.

▶ Mix the peanut sauce ingredients together well in a bowl.

▶ Bring a large pan of water to the boil and add the noodles. Cook for 3 minutes, then rinse and drain. Toss in the 2 tespoons of sesame oil, then divide the noodles among four plates.

▶ Top the noodles with chicken and cucumber and pour over the peanut sauce. Serve immediately.

Five-spice Pork with Noodles

This can also be made with skinless chicken breasts or a vegetarian substitute such as bean curd.

450 g/1 lb lean, boneless pork, thinly sliced
½ tsp five-spice powder
Salt and freshly ground black pepper
2 spring onions, finely chopped
1 clove garlic, crushed
225 g/8 oz dried egg noodles
3 Tbsp peanut oil
225 g/8 oz tinned bamboo shoots
225 g/8 oz mange tout, trimmed
3 Tbsp Japanese soy sauce or Chinese light soy sauce
2 Tbsp toasted sesame seeds (see page 18)

▶ Mix the pork with the five-spice powder, seasoning, spring onions and garlic. Cover, refrigerate and leave to marinate for two hours.

▶ Place the noodles in a pan and pour over boiling water to cover. Bring back to the boil and cook for 2 minutes, then drain and rinse under cold water. Leave to drain.

▶ In a wok or frying pan, heat the oil and stir-fry the pork until well browned. Add the sliced bamboo shoots and peas, and stir-fry for 3 to 4 minutes, or until the vegetables are cooked. Push the mixture to one side of the wok and add the noodles. Stir-fry the noodles for 2 minutes to heat through, then stir in the reserved mixture, soy sauce and sesame seeds. Stir-fry for 1 minute before serving.

Red Chilli Chicken Noodles

The luscious red sauce that coats the noodles gives this dish a fiery look to equal its fiery taste. If your palate prefers something less challenging, reduce the amount of chilli oil and fresh chilli, and seed the chilli before use.

225 g/8 oz dried, thin egg noodles
225 g/8 oz boneless, skinless chicken breast, finely sliced
Oil for stir-frying
1 Tbsp peanut oil
1 tsp five-spice powder
1 tsp chilli powder
2 cloves garlic, crushed
2 Tbsp Japanese soy sauce or Chinese light soy sauce
1 tsp chilli oil
2 Tbsp tomato purée
2 tsp granulated brown sugar
4 spring onions, sliced
50 g/2 oz tinned bamboo shoots, drained
1 red chilli, chopped

▶ Place the noodles in a pan and pour over boiling water to cover. Bring back to the boil and cook for 2 minutes, then drain.

▶ Heat a little frying oil in a wok or frying pan and stir-fry the chicken for 3 to 4 minutes or until cooked. Remove with a slotted spoon onto kitchen paper. Discard the oil and wipe the wok with kitchen paper.

▶ Heat the peanut oil in the wok and cook the spices, chilli powder, garlic and soy sauce for 30 seconds. Drain the noodles and add to the wok with the remaining ingredients. Stir in the chicken and cook for 4 to 5 minutes. Serve immediately.

Japanese Stir-fry Steamed Noodles (*Yakisoba*)

This is one of the most popular noodle dishes in Japan and is always on the menu of street vendors. If you cannot buy *yakisoba* sauce, you can substitute Japanese brown sauce or make your own.

600 g/1¼ lb Japanese steamed noodles, or 325 g/11 oz dried egg noodles
1 Tbsp sesame oil
2 Tbsp sunflower oil
225 g/8 oz boneless, skinless chicken breasts, thinly sliced
1 medium onion, sliced
75 g/3 oz halved and thinly sliced carrots
5 cabbage leaves, roughly chopped
Salt and freshly ground black pepper
7 Tbsp *yakisoba* sauce
½ sheet seaweed paper, shredded
Red pickled ginger (*beni-shoga*) (optional)

▶ If using Japanese steamed noodles, just rinse. If using dried noodles, bring a saucepan of water to the boil, add the noodles and cook for 3 minutes. Rinse under cold water and drain. Toss in the sesame oil.

▶ Heat the sunflower oil in a wok or frying pan, then fry the chicken for 3 to 4 minutes. Add the onion, carrot and cabbage and stir-fry for 3 to 4 minutes. Season then stir in the noodles and *yakisoba* sauce.

▶ Divide the noodles among four plates and sprinkle with seaweed and pickled ginger. Serve immediately.

yakisoba sauce

5 Tbsp brown sauce
4 Tbsp Japanese soy sauce
4 tsp tomato ketchup
4 tsp oyster sauce
4 Tbsp caster sugar

▶ Mix all the ingredients together in a small bowl. Cover and chill. Use within 24 hours.

Indonesian Soft Noodles with Vegetables

This dish (*Gado gado*) is traditionally served as a cold salad.

75 g/3 oz green cabbage, sliced
200 g/7 oz bean sprouts
75 g/3 oz green beans
50 g/2 oz matchstick-cut carrots
400 g/14 oz fresh, thin egg noodles, or
300 g/10 oz dried, thin egg noodles
1 Tbsp sesame oil

peanut sauce

1 Tbsp vegetable oil
1 clove garlic, crushed
1 shallot, finely chopped
½ tsp chilli powder
500 ml/1 pt water
1 Tbsp granulated brown sugar
8 Tbsp chunky peanut butter
Pinch of salt
Juice of ½ lemon

▶ To make the sauce, heat the oil in a wok or frying pan, and stir-fry the garlic and shallot for 1 minute. Add the chilli powder, water, sugar and peanut butter. Stir well. Add the salt and lemon juice, stir and simmer gently.
▶ Bring a saucepan of water to the boil and blanch the cabbage, bean sprouts, beans and carrots for 2 to 3 minutes. Drain well.
▶ Bring water to the boil and cook the noodles for 3 minutes. Rinse under cold water and drain well. Toss with sesame oil and divide among four plates. Top with the vegetables and pour over the peanut sauce to serve.

Prawns with Black Bean Sauce and Noodles

Chinese black bean sauce has a distinctive, strong, salty taste.

300 g/10 oz dried, medium egg noodles
2 Tbsp vegetable oil
2.5-centimetre/1-inch piece root ginger, peeled and finely chopped
3 cloves garlic, crushed
125 g/4 oz small cooked prawns, shelled
12 large cooked prawns, shelled and deveined
1 small red pepper, sliced
4 spring onions, chopped into 2.5-centimetre/1-inch lengths
Freshly ground black pepper
1 Tbsp sesame oil
4 tsp Chinese light soy sauce
4 tsp Chinese dark soy sauce
2 Tbsp sweet rice wine or dry sherry
3 Tbsp black bean sauce

▶ Bring a saucepan of water to the boil, add the noodles and cook for 4 minutes. Rinse under cold water and drain.
▶ Heat the vegetable oil in a wok or frying pan, and stir-fry the ginger and garlic for 30 seconds. Add the prawns, pepper, spring onion and pepper to taste and stir-fry for 2 minutes. Stir in the sesame oil and noodles then add the remaining ingredients and stir well.
▶ Divide the noodles and prawns among four plates to serve.

Chinese Vegetable Noodle Stir-fry (Chow Mein)

Packed full of fresh vegetables, this dish is ideal for vegetarians.

300 g/10 oz dried, medium egg noodles
2 Tbsp vegetable oil
2.5-centimetre/1-inch piece root ginger, peeled and finely chopped
2 cloves garlic, crushed
300 g/10 oz Chinese leaves, chopped into bite-sized squares
200 g/7 oz bean sprouts
1 small red pepper, cut into bite-sized squares
1 small green pepper, cut into bite-sized squares
16 tinned straw mushrooms, halved
1 Tbsp sesame oil
2 spring onions, chopped
4 Tbsp Chinese light soy sauce
1 Tbsp Chinese dark soy sauce
1 Tbsp caster sugar
Salt and freshly ground black pepper

▶ Bring a large saucepan of water to the boil, add the noodles and cook for 3 to 4 minutes. Rinse under cold water and drain.

▶ Heat the vegetable oil in a wok or frying pan, and stir-fry the ginger and garlic for 30 seconds. Stir in each ingredient as you add the Chinese leaves, bean sprouts, peppers and mushrooms. Fry together for about 2 minutes. Stir in the remaining ingredients to heat through and season to taste. Divide the noodles and vegetables among four plates and serve immediately.

Spicy Noodles with Beef and Vegetables

The shrimp paste used in this dish is highly pungent, but do not let the odour put you off. Wise Malaysian and Thai cooks make sure their kitchen is well-ventilated while it is being cooked.

300 g/10 oz dried, medium egg noodles
3 Tbsp vegetable oil
2 to 3 small dried red chillies, soaked in hot water, then ground
2 cloves garlic, finely chopped
1 tsp dried shrimp paste (optional)
300 g/10 oz rump steak, thinly sliced
1 medium onion, thinly sliced
2 green chillies, chopped
200 g/7 oz bean sprouts
125 g/4 oz fresh spinach
Salt and freshly ground black pepper
3 Tbsp Japanese soy sauce and Chinese light soy sauce
Coriander leaves
4 lime wedges

▶ Bring a large saucepan of water to the boil, add the noodles and cook for 4 minutes. Rinse under cold water and drain.

▶ Heat the oil in a wok or frying pan, and stir-fry the red chillies, garlic and shrimp paste. Add the beef and fry for 2 to 3 minutes or until cooked.

▶ Stir in each ingredient as you add the onion, green chillies, bean sprouts and spinach. Season to taste with the salt and pepper.

▶ Add the noodles, sprinkle with soy sauce, and mix well. Divide the noodles among four plates and then garnish with coriander and lime wedges. Serve immediately.

Curried Vegetable Noodles

Curried vegetables are tossed into egg noodles for a very quick vegetarian dish. Use any combination of vegetables that will provide interesting textures and colours.

300 g/10 oz dried egg noodles
3 Tbsp peanut oil
1 small aubergine, sliced and quartered
1 courgette, sliced
375 g/12 oz fresh baby corn, sliced
2 cloves garlic, crushed
1 onion, halved and sliced
50 g/2 oz okra, scored around the top
300 ml/10 fl oz coconut milk
¼ tsp turmeric
1 tsp chilli powder
Curry powder to taste
1 tsp granulated brown sugar
2 Tbsp Japanese soy sauce or Chinese light soy sauce
2 Tbsp chopped coriander

▶ Boil the noodles following the instructions on the packet. Drain and sprinkle with a little oil.
▶ Heat the oil in a large pan and cook the aubergine, courgette, corn, garlic, onion and okra for 5 minutes. Stir in the coconut milk, spices, curry powder, sugar and soy sauce, and simmer for 5 minutes. Warm a serving dish.
▶ Place the noodles in the serving dish, and spoon over the curried vegetables. Serve immediately.

Simple Garlic Noodles

The healthy properties of garlic are widely acknowledged, so do not recoil at the quantity of garlic used in this flavoursome, winter-warming dish.

1 Tbsp sesame oil
16 cloves garlic, sliced
1 lb *ramen* noodles, or 325 g/11 oz thin, dried egg noodles
4 cloves garlic, crushed
1.4 L/2½ pt Soy Sauce Broth (see page 23)
4 Tbsp cooked, dried bamboo shoots (optional)
2 spring onions, chopped

▶ Heat the oil in a frying pan, and fry the sliced garlic for 2 to 3 minutes, or until golden brown. Remove and set aside.
▶ Bring a large saucepan of water to the boil. Add the noodles and cook for 3 minutes. Drain and divide the noodles among four bowls.
▶ Put the crushed garlic and broth in a pan, bring to the boil, then simmer for 2 to 3 minutes. Remove the garlic and reserve the broth. Arrange the fried garlic, bamboo shoots and spring onions on the noodles and pour over the broth. Serve immediately.

rice noodles

chapter 2

Thai Hot and Sour Noodle Soup with Prawns (Tom Yam Goong)

This is one of the most exquisite dishes of Thai cuisine. The broth is a myriad of texture and flavours – sour lime leaves and lemon grass, spicy ginger and chillies and sweet seafood.

1 Tbsp vegetable oil
2 cloves garlic, finely chopped
2 shallots, finely chopped
1-centimetre/½-inch piece root ginger, sliced thin
4 to 5 small red chillies, chopped
1.4 L/2½ pt Light Chicken Stock (see page 23)
3 Kaffir lime leaves, sliced
10-centimetre/4-inch piece lemonl grass, chopped
200 g/7 oz rice vermicelli
20 large cooked prawns, shelled and deveined
6 Tbsp fish sauce
6 Tbsp fresh lemon or lime juice
2 Tbsp granulated brown sugar
16 tinned straw mushrooms
Fresh coriander leaves

▶ Heat the oil in a pan. When hot, stir-fry the garlic, shallots, ginger and chillies for 1 minute. Pour in the stock, then add the lime leaves and lemon grass. Bring to the boil and simmer for 5 minutes.

▶ Meanwhile, soak the noodles for 3 minutes in warm water, drain and rinse under cold water. Drain before dividing the noodles among four bowls. Add the prawns, fish sauce, lemon juice, sugar and mushrooms to the stock and simmer for 3 minutes. Pour over the noodles and sprinkle with coriander.

Malaysian Coconut Prawn Noodle Soup (Laksa Lemak)

A Malaysian soup famous throughout the culinary world for its silky, smooth texture and spicy bite.

8 spring onions, sliced
3 cloves garlic, sliced
2.5-centimetre/1-inch piece root ginger, peeled and sliced
4 small red chillies, sliced
1 Tbsp chopped lemon grass
5 Tbsp vegetable oil
2 tsp turmeric
1 tsp ground coriander
2 tsp dried shrimp paste (optional)
125 g/4 oz bean curd, drained and diced
850 ml/1½ pt Light Chicken Stock (see page 23)
600 ml/1 pt tinned coconut milk
2 tsp granulated sugar
2 tsp salt
2 cooked fish balls (see page 27), sliced into rounds
200 g/7 oz rice vermicelli
12 large cooked prawns, shelled and deveined

garnish

225 g/8 oz skinless, cooked chicken, finely chopped
400 g/14 oz bean sprouts
5-centimetre/2-inch piece of cucumber, finely chopped
1 large red chilli, sliced
2 spring onions, chopped

▶ Blend the spring onions, garlic, ginger, chillies and lemon grass in a food processor. Heat 3 tablespoons of the oil in a pan and stir-fry the spring onion mixture with the turmeric, coriander and shrimp paste over low heat for 4 minutes.

▶ Heat the remaining oil in a frying pan and fry the bean curd until light brown. Add the stock, coconut milk, sugar, salt and fish balls. Bring to the boil, then simmer for 3 minutes. Blanch the bean sprouts in boiling water for I minute.

▶ Soak the noodles in warm water for 3 minutes, then drain and rinse under cold water. Drain again before dividing the noodles among four bowls.

▶ Add the prawns to the bean curd and stock mixture, and simmer for 2 minutes. Spoon over the noodles and top with small amounts of the garnishes. Serve immediately.

Thai Pork and Noodle Soup (Kwitiaow Nam)

This Thai soup is served from floating kitchens working up and down rivers and canals. This version contains three varieties of pork. Preserved cabbage and fish balls can be bought at Chinese or specialist food shops.

200 g/7 oz lean pork loin, thinly sliced
325 g/11 oz dried, rice stick noodles
300 g/10 oz bean sprouts
125 g/4 oz pig's liver, boiled and thinly sliced
1 tsp chopped preserved cabbage (optional)
1.8 L/3¼ pt Chicken Stock (see page 22)
12 fish balls (see page 27)
125 g/4 oz minced lean pork
1 spring onion, chopped
2 Tbsp coarsely chopped coriander leaves and stems
2 Tbsp chopped garlic, fried in oil until golden
½ tsp ground white pepper

▶ Boil the pork loin in water for about 15 minutes. Allow to cool before cutting into 1-centimetre/½-inch wide strips. Cover and set aside.

▶ In a pan, boil water to cover the noodles and bean sprouts. Add the noodles and bean sprouts and boil for 3 minutes. Drain and divide among deep bowls. Top with the pork loin, pig's liver and preserved cabbage.

▶ Bring the stock to the boil. Add the fish balls and boil for 3 minutes. Remove with a slotted spoon and add to the bowls. Reserve the stock.

▶ Put the ground pork in a pan with 350 ml/12 fl oz of the Chicken Stock. Heat gently and stir until the pork is cooked, about 4 to 5 minutes. Stir in the spring onions, coriander, garlic and pepper to heat through. Ladle the pork mixture and stock into the bowls. Top with more heated Chicken Stock to fill each bowl. Serve immediately.

Cold Noodles with Vegetables (*Kuksu*)

This popular noodle dish is served with side dishes like soy sauce, cayenne pepper or Korean chilli powder, and pickled vegetables.

3 Tbsp Japanese soy sauce
3 tsp sugar
1 Tbsp sesame oil
5 dried *shiitake* mushrooms, soaked for 20 minutes in hot water
125 g/4 oz bean sprouts
450 g/1 lb young, fresh spinach leaves, stalks removed
450 ml/16 fl oz Vegetable Stock (see page 23)
225 g/8 oz rice vermicelli noodles
Green part of 1 spring onion, sliced diagonally
1 Tbsp toasted sesame seeds (see page 18), crushed
Small pinch cayenne pepper

▶ Mix together 2 tablespoons of the soy sauce, 2 teaspoons of the sugar and all of the sesame oil.

▶ Drain the *shiitake* mushrooms and remove the stalks and woody parts. Thinly slice the caps.

▶ Bring 700 ml/1¼ pt water to the boil in a pan and add the remaining sugar. Put the bean sprouts in a small metal colander and lower into the water. Bring back to the boil and cook the bean sprouts for 20 seconds, then remove. Reserve the water. Rinse the bean sprouts under cold water and leave to drain.

▶ Boil the spinach in the reserved water until wilted. Drain, rinse under cold water and drain again. Discard the water.

▶ Pour the stock into a pan and add the remaining soy sauce. Bring to the boil, then add the noodles and cook until just tender. Remove the noodles using a slotted spoon and put into the serving dish. Add the spinach and mushrooms to the stock. Heat through then quickly remove, reserving the stock. Pile onto the noodles and season with a little of the soy sauce mixture.

▶ Heat the bean sprouts in the stock, then remove and pile onto the spinach and mushrooms. Season with the remaining soy sauce mixture. Pour the stock around the noodles and sprinkle over the remaining ingredients to serve.

Vietnamese Rice Stick Noodles

You can make a store of roasted chilli flakes – used here to garnish – by roasting 125 g/4 oz red chillies in a hot oven (400°F/200°C/Gas mark 6) until brown. Lightly blend in a food processor to produce flakes and store in an airtight container. Pickled radish is sold in packets and jars at Asian food shops.

2 Tbsp vegetable oil
2 cloves garlic, finely chopped
125 g/4 oz lean, boneless pork, sliced
4 large fresh prawns, shelled and deveined, tails intact
1 Tbsp dried prawns
2 Tbsp pickled white radish, finely chopped (optional)
50 g/2 oz diced bean curd
3 Tbsp lemon juice
3 Tbsp fish sauce
3 Tbsp granulated sugar
175 g/6 oz thick, rice stick noodles, soaked in warm water for about 5 minutes, and drained
2 eggs, beaten
75 g/3 oz bean sprouts
3 Tbsp crushed salted peanuts
2 Tbsp chopped spring onions
2 Tbsp chopped coriander
½ tsp roasted chilli flakes (see above)
4 lemon wedges

▶ Heat the oil in a wok or frying pan and stir-fry the garlic until golden brown. Increase the heat and add the pork, and fry for 6 minutes or until cooked. Add the prawns, dried prawns and pickled radish, and continue stir-frying for 1 minute. Add the bean curd and stir gently, then reduce the heat and stir in the lemon juice, fish sauce and sugar. Cook for 3 minutes.

▶ Add the noodles and stir the mixture for 1 to 2 minutes. Push to one side and add the eggs. Once they begin to set, stir to scramble them.

▶ Warm a large serving plate.

▶ Top the noodle mixture with the bean sprouts, peanuts, spring onions and coriander. Stir to combine with the scrambled eggs, and spoon onto the serving plate.

▶ Serve with extra bean sprouts, crushed peanuts, chopped coriander, roasted chilli flakes and lemon wedges.

Thai White Noodle Nests with Sauce (Khanom Chiin Nam Yaa)

The basis of this meal-in-a-bowl is a nest of long rice noodles.

chilli paste

125 g/4 oz shallots, finely chopped
1 Tbsp chopped garlic
4 anchovy fillets
225 ml/8 fl oz water
2 Tbsp sliced root ginger
2 Tbsp sliced lemon grass
1 dried red chilli, seeded
1 tsp dried shrimp paste (optional)
Pinch of salt

noodles and sauce

200 g/7 oz white fish fillets, skinned
225 g/8 oz dried vermicelli, soaked for 3 to 5 minutes
700 ml/1¼ pt coconut milk
700 ml/1¼ pt Chicken Stock (see page 22)
20 fish balls (see page 27) (optional)
3 Tbsp fish sauce
125 g/4 oz bean sprouts, blanched
75 g/3 oz chopped green beans
125 g/4 oz spinach, blanched
75 g/3 oz lemon basil leaves

▶ Mix the chilli paste ingredients in a wok or pan, then cook over medium heat for 1 minute. Allow to cool and process to a paste in a food processor. Cover.

▶ Boil the green beans in water for 3 to 4 minutes, drain then set aside.

▶ Boil the fish in a small amount of water for 10 minutes. Remove with a slotted spoon and, when cool, finely chop.

▶ Place the noodles in a pan and pour over boiling water to cover. Bring back to the boil and cook for 5 minutes, then drain. When cool, fold the noodles into four serving bowls.

▶ In a pan, heat the coconut milk and Chicken Stock, then add the chilli paste, fish, fish balls and fish sauce, and boil for 3 minutes. Remove from the heat and spoon over the noodles. Serve with small dishes of bean sprouts, beans, spinach and lemon basil leaves.

Black Bean Noodles with Bean Curd

Nutritious and healthy as it undoubtedly is, bean curd will never win any awards for flavour, which is why combining it with the spicy and aromatic black bean sauce works so well.

300 g/10 oz dried rice stick noodles
4 Tbsp vegetable oil
350 g/12 oz bean curd, diced
2.5-centimetres/1-inch piece root ginger, peeled and finely chopped
2 cloves garlic, crushed
½ green pepper, diced
½ red pepper, diced
½ yellow pepper, diced
5 spring onions, chopped
6 Tbsp black bean sauce
3 Tbsp Chinese light soy sauce
2 Tbsp Chinese rice wine or dry sherry
2 tsp caster sugar

▶ Soak the noodles in warm water for 2 to 5 minutes, depending on the instructions on the packet. Rinse under cold water and drain.

▶ Heat 3 tablespoons of the oil in a wok or frying pan, and fry the bean curd until golden brown. Stir in the ginger and garlic. Add the peppers and spring onions and stir-fry for 1 to 2 minutes.

▶ Add the noodles and the remaining oil and ingredients. Stir until the noodles are well coated with sauce. Divide the noodles among four plates and serve immediately.

Singapore Spicy Noodles

Although the origins of this curry-flavoured dish lie in India, Singapore has been the cultural melting pot where most Chinese migrants have come into contact with Indian cuisine.

225 g/8 oz rice vermicelli noodles
3 Tbsp vegetable oil
2 cloves garlic, crushed
1-centimetre/½-inch piece root ginger, peeled and finely chopped
1 red chilli, chopped
125 g/4 oz cooked prawns, shelled and deveined
6 small squid, cleaned and sliced
225 g/8 oz bean sprouts
400 g/14 oz fresh spinach, blanched
225 g/8 oz Chinese barbecued pork (*cha siu*) (see page 16), thinly sliced
2 eggs, beaten
3 spring onions, roughly chopped
⅔ tsp salt
Pinch of chilli powder
Freshly ground black pepper
2 to 3 tsp hot curry powder
1 Tbsp Japanese soy sauce or Chinese light soy sauce
2 tsp caster sugar
150 ml/5 fl oz Chicken Stock (see page 22)

- Soak the noodles in warm water for 3 to 5 minutes. Rinse under cold water and drain.
- Heat 3 tablespoons of the oil in a wok or frying pan until very hot, and stir-fry the garlic, ginger and red chilli for 30 seconds.
- Add the prawns and squid and stir-fry for 1 minute. Add in the bean sprouts, spinach and pork and stir-fry for 1 to 2 minutes.
- Make a well in the middle, and pour in the egg. Scramble lightly, then quickly stir in the noodles.
- Add the remaining ingredients and stir until the sauce is absorbed. Divide the noodles among four plates and serve immediately.

Thai-fried Noodles with Chicken *(Pad Thai)*

A vegetarian version of this dish – minus the chicken and substituting vegetable for Chicken Stock – loses none of the taste. This meal can be bulked-out with additional bean curd. See page 54 for an alternate version of *Pad Thai* which uses prawns.

sauce

225 ml/8 fl oz water
125 ml/4 fl oz tamarind juice
5 Tbsp granulated sugar
1 Tbsp Chinese light soy sauce

noodles

325 g/11 oz dried rice noodles
3 Tbsp peanut or corn oil
175 g/6 oz boneless, skinless chicken breast, finely sliced
1-centimetre/½-inch piece root ginger, finely chopped
2 cloves garlic, finely chopped
1 red chilli, chopped
125 g/4 oz bean curd, diced
4 eggs
50 ml/2 fl oz Chicken Stock (see page 22)
3 Tbsp sliced shallots
3 Tbsp dried prawns, chopped
5 Tbsp unsalted peanuts, chopped
4 spring onions, sliced
425 g/15 oz bean sprouts
Slices of lemon, to garnish
Slices of cucumber, to garnish
Coriander leaves, to garnish

▶ Soak the noodles in hot water for 7 to 10 minutes, drain and set aside.

▶ Mix the sauce ingredients together in a pan and boil until reduced to about 150 ml/5 fl oz. Set aside to cool.

▶ Drain the noodles. Heat the oil in a wok until it just starts to smoke, and stir-fry the chicken for 3 minutes. Add the ginger, garlic and chilli, and stir-fry for 1 minute. Add the bean curd and stir-fry for 1 minute, then break in the eggs. Stir-fry for 1 more minute then add the noodles and stock. When the noodles are soft, add the remaining ingredients and the sauce, and stir-fry for 2 minutes. Garnish with the lemon and cucumber slices and coriander.

Hot and Sour Red Vermicelli

Red curry paste in this Thai dish shows the influence of China and India. The result is an interesting combination of heat and sourness.

225 g/8 oz rice vermicelli noodles
3 Tbsp vegetable oil
225 g/8 oz bean curd, diced
3 cloves garlic, chopped
125 g/4 oz tinned sliced bamboo shoots
225 g/8 oz bean sprouts
125 g/4 oz fresh spinach, blanched
2 Tbsp red curry paste
6 Tbsp fish sauce
3 Tbsp Chinese light soy sauce
1 Tbsp granulated brown sugar
Coriander leaves
4 lime wedges

▶ Soak the noodles in warm water for 3 to 5 minutes, then rinse under cold water and drain.
▶ Heat the oil in a wok or frying pan and fry the bean curd until golden brown. Stir in the garlic, bamboo shoots, bean sprouts and spinach.
▶ Add the red curry paste, fish sauce, soy sauce, and sugar, and stir well. Add the noodles and stir until well coated with sauce.
▶ Divide the noodles among four plates and sprinkle over the coriander. Serve immediately with lime wedges.

Vietnamese Vegetable Stir-fry with Noodles (Mí Bùn Xào Vói Rau Dâu)

This basic stir-fry uses a minimum of ingredients to achieve maximum flavour. Change the vegetables to match seasonal specialties, and for extra spice sprinkle over roasted chilli flakes (see page 44).

1 Tbsp vegetable oil
1 clove garlic, finely chopped
1 carrot, thinly sliced
50 ml/2 fl oz water
1 small head Chinese leaves, shredded
½ celery stalk, grated
3 Tbsp Chicken Stock (see page 22)
1 Tbsp oyster sauce
1 Tbsp fish sauce
1 tsp granulated sugar
Freshly ground black pepper
225 g/8 oz rice vermicelli noodles, soaked in warm water for 5 minutes, and drained

▶ Heat the oil in a wok or skillet over a high heat and fry the garlic until golden brown. Add the carrot and stir-fry for 1 minute.
▶ Add the remaining ingredients except the noodles, and cook for 2 minutes, stirring gently.
▶ Add the noodles and toss to combine all the ingredients. Stir for 1 minute then serve immediately.

Chinese Liver and Chive Vermicelli

This Chinese dish is usually served as a light lunch. As the liver is marinated in rice wine and soy sauce it develops new flavours. Even though chicken livers are used in this recipe, they can be replaced by another type of liver.

225 g/8 oz rice vermicelli noodles
450 g/1 lb chicken livers, sliced
2 tsp light soy sauce
1 tsp Chinese rice wine or dry sherry
1 Tbsp cornflour
3 Tbsp vegetable oil
2 cloves garlic, very finely chopped
2.5-centimetre/1-inch piece root ginger, peeled and very finely chopped
225 g/8 oz bean sprouts
225 g/8 dried *shiitake* mushrooms, soaked in hot water, stalks removed, then sliced
225 g/8 oz spring onions, cut into 5-centimetre/2-inch lengths
Salt

sauce

1 Tbsp sesame oil
4 Tbsp Chicken Stock (see page 22)
1 Tbsp Chinese rice wine or dry sherry
2½ Tbsp Chinese light soy sauce
4 tsp Chinese dark soy sauce
2 tsp oyster sauce
1 tsp caster sugar
Freshly ground black pepper

▶ Soak the noodles in warm water for 3 minutes. Rinse under cold water and drain.

▶ Blanch the chicken livers in boiling water until they turn white, then marinate in the soy sauce, rice wine and cornflour for 20 minutes.

▶ Heat 2 tablespoons of the oil in a wok or frying pan, and stir-fry the liver for 3 to 4 minutes before stirring in the garlic and ginger. Add the remaining tablespoon of oil and the bean sprouts, mushrooms and spring onions and stir-fry for 1 to 2 minutes.

▶ Add the sauce ingredients and noodles, and stir over heat until the sauce is absorbed. Add salt to taste. Divide the noodles and livers among four plates and serve immediately.

Fresh Spinach Noodle Salad

Fresh, young spinach leaves should be used for this innovative recipe. The small dark green leaves look as good as they taste, and they are packed with nutrients.

225 g/8 oz dried rice stick noodles
1 Tbsp peanut oil
8 spring onions, sliced
2 cloves garlic, crushed
½ tsp ground star anise
2 tsp chopped root ginger
2 Tbsp dark soy sauce
1 Tbsp sesame oil
75 g/3 oz young spinach leaves, washed
2 Tbsp chopped coriander

▶ Bring a pan of water to the boil and boil the noodles for 4 to 5 minutes. Rinse under cold water and drain.

▶ Heat the peanut oil in a wok or frying pan and cook half of the spring onions and all of the garlic, star anise, ginger and soy sauce for 2 minutes. Remove with a slotted spoon onto kitchen paper to drain and cool.

▶ In a bowl, toss together the noodles and the spring onion mixture, and sprinkle over the sesame oil. Arrange the spinach in a serving bowl and top with the noodle mixture and vegetables. Garnish with the remaining spring onions and the coriander to serve.

Brunch Eggs and Rice Noodles (Bún Xào Trúng)

Black jack is a traditional Vietnamese ingredient. If you cannot buy it, make your own by heating 1 tablespoon of sugar in a wok or frying pan until it darkens. Remove from the heat and very carefully stir in 2 tablespoons of cold water.

225 g/8 oz rice vermicelli noodles
1 tsp black jack
2 cloves garlic, crushed
2 spring onions, chopped
Salt and freshly ground black pepper
6 eggs, beaten
1 iceberg lettuce, shredded
½ cucumber, sliced
2 Tbsp pickled carrot or dill pickle
1 Tbsp chopped spearmint leaves
1 Tbsp chopped coriander
1 Tbsp vegetable oil

sauce

1 clove garlic, roughly chopped
1 red chilli, roughly chopped
1 Tbsp fish sauce
1 tsp lemon juice
1 Tbsp granulated sugar

▶ Bring a large pan of lightly salted water to the boil, and boil the noodles, stirring constantly, for about 3 minutes. Drain and rinse under cold water. Drain again and set aside.

▶ To make the sauce, grind the garlic and chilli together in a food processor. Transfer to a small bowl and stir in the remaining sauce ingredients. Mix thoroughly to dissolve the sugar. Cover and set aside.

▶ Combine the black jack, garlic and spring onions in a shallow dish. Season, and then add the eggs. Mix well and set aside to marinate for 5 minutes

▶ Arrange the lettuce, cucumber, pickled carrots, mint and coriander into four bowls. Top each with the noodles, and set aside.

▶ Heat the oil in a wok or frying pan and pour in the egg mixture. Flip it once, then remove and allow to cool for 1 to 2 minutes. Cut into 8 pieces, and put 2 pieces in each bowl. Spoon over the sauce to serve.

Vietnamese Chicken Noodle Soup (Pho Gà)

A perfect brunch or late-night snack sold all over Vietnam by street vendors. Once a meal like this would have been based around beef, but modern versions use chicken or prawns.

3 celery sticks, finely chopped
3 spring onions with green tops, chopped into rings
300 g/10 oz cooked chicken, skinned and cut into fine strips
2 pieces light wood ear fungus, or 225 g/8 white button mushrooms
225 g/8 oz steamed flat rice noodles, or dried rice stick noodles
850 ml/1½ pt Chicken Stock (see page 23)
Salt

▶ Place the celery and spring onions in a bowl, and the chicken in another bowl. Place both on the table. If using wood ear fungus, soak it in hot water for 20 to 30 minutes.

▶ Cook the noodles following the instructions on the packet. Rinse and drain then divide the noodles between four bowls.

▶ In a pan, bring the stock to a simmer and add the wood ear fungi and salt. Cook for 3 to 5 minutes. Pour into a bowl and place on the table.

▶ To eat, place celery, spring onions and chicken onto the noodles, and ladle on the chicken and mushroom stock.

Thai-fried Noodles with Prawns (*Pad Thai*)

This is the best-known of all Thai noodle dishes. The key to a tasty *Pad Thai* lies in the use of salty dried prawns and roasted peanuts. Adjust the amount of chilli used to suit your palate. See page 48 for an alternate version of this popular Thai dish which uses chicken.

12 large cooked prawns, shelled and deveined, tails intact
300 g/10 oz dried rice stick noodles
4 Tbsp vegetable oil
3 cloves garlic, crushed
4 shallots, sliced
2 eggs, beaten
2 Tbsp roasted peanuts, crushed
3 to 4 small green chillies, chopped
2 Tbsp dried prawns, chopped
2 spring onions, chopped
200 g/7 oz bean sprouts
2½ Tbsp granulated brown sugar
6 Tbsp fish sauce
125 ml/4 fl oz fresh lemon juice
Corinader leaves
4 lime wedges

marinade

1 tsp freshly squeezed lemon juice
1 tsp fish sauce
½ tsp granulated brown sugar

▶ Mix together the marinade ingredients and marinate the prawns for at least 15 minutes.

▶ Soak the noodles in warm water for 2 to 5 minutes, or according to the instructions on the packet. Rinse under cold water and drain.

▶ Heat 2 tablespoons of the oil in a wok or frying pan, and stir-fry the garlic and spring onions for 30 seconds. Make a well in the middle and pour in the eggs. Lightly scramble without incorporating the garlic and shallots. Stir in the peanuts, chillies, dried prawns, spring onions and bean sprouts.

▶ Add 1 tablespoon of oil to the wok, and stir in the noodles. Add the sugar, fish sauce and lemon juice, and stir to coat the noodles. Push to one side while the marinated prawns are stir-fried in the remaining tablespoon of oil.

▶ Divide the noodles among four plates and top with the prawns, coriander leaves and lime wedges. Serve immediately.

wheat & buckwheat noodles

chapter 3

Fried Prawns with Noodles *(Tempura Soba)*

Nowhere it is written that a healthy meal cannot be a gourmet experience. This simple *tempura* dish proves the point – it is both nutritious and delicious.

Oil for deep frying
1 egg, beaten
4 Tbsp plain flour
125 ml/4 fl oz water
4 large fresh prawns, shelled and deveined
Plain flour for coating
8 fresh *shiitake* mushrooms
400 g/14 oz dried *soba* noodles
1.4 L/1½ pt Japanese Broth (see page 24)

▶ Fill a pan one-third full of oil and heat to 350°F/175°C.Check the temperature by dropping in some batter or a piece of bread; if it bubbles and floats to the surface, the oil is at the right temperature.

▶ To make the batter, mix the egg, flour and water lightly in a bowl. The batter should be quite lumpy with some flour visible on top of the mixture.

▶ Coat the prawns with flour and dip into the batter to cover. Dip the mushrooms into the batter.

▶ Deep-fry the prawns and mushrooms until golden brown. Set aside on kitchen paper to drain.

▶ Bring a large pan of water to the boil and add the noodles. Cook for 5 minutes, then drain and rinse under cold water. Divide the noodles among four bowls.

▶ In a pan, bring the broth to the boil and pour it over the noodles. Top each bowl with one prawn and two mushrooms. Serve immediately.

Japanese Noodle Stir-Fry (Sukiyaki Udon)

In many Japanese homes, the noodles are cooked with the steak and vegetables to absorb the delicious flavours.

175 ml/6 fl oz Premier Japanese Stock (see page 24)
1½ Tbsp granulated sugar
2 Tbsp rice wine
2½ Tbsp Japanese soy sauce
2 spring onions, chopped
350 g/12 oz rump steak, thinly sliced
½–1 leek, sliced diagonally
4 to 6 Chinese leaves, chopped
4 fresh *shiitake* mushrooms, halved
600 g/1¼ lb parboiled, fresh *udon* noodles or 450 g/1 lb dried *udon*
1.4 L/2½ pt Japanese Broth (see page 24)

▶ Put the stock, sugar, rice wine and soy sauce into a pan and bring to the boil. Add the steak, leek, Chinese leaves and mushrooms, then simmer for 7 to 10 minutes. Set aside.
▶ Bring water to the boil, add the noodles and boil for 3 minutes. Drain, rinse with cold water, then drain again.
▶ Add the noodles to the vegetable mixture (the *sukiyaki*), and stir-fry for 2 to 3 minutes. Serve immediately.

Curry Sauce Noodles (Kare Udon)

A modern Japanese recipe combining the spicy flavour of a curry sauce with the smooth texture of *udon* noodles.

600 g/1¼ lb parboiled *udon* noodles or 450 g/1 lb dried *udon*
1.25 L/2¼ pt Japanese Broth (see page 24)

curry

1 Tbsp vegetable oil
2 boneless, skinless chicken breasts, diced
1 medium onion, sliced
2 Tbsp plain flour
1 to 2 tsp curry powder
½ chicken stock cube
300 ml/10 fl oz water
2 Tbsp fruit relish
75 g/3 oz dried currants
Salt and pepper

▶ Heat the oil and fry the chicken until cooked through. Push aside, and fry the onion until lightly browned. Add the flour and curry powder and fry for 1 to 2 minutes.
▶ In a pan, dissolve the stock cube in the water. Add the relish, currants and seasonings. Simmer for 10 minutes, then stir in the chicken.
▶ Bring water to the boil and cook the noodles for 3 minutes. Rinse under cold water and drain. Divide among four serving bowls. Meanwhile, heat the broth. Pour the curry sauce over the noodles and then pour over the broth to serve.

Bean Curd Sheets with Noodles (*Kitsune Udon*)

This is one of Japan's classic noodle dishes. Deep-fried sheets of bean curd are available from specialist shops. They can be stored in the freezer for long periods.

600 g/1¼ lb parboiled fresh *udon* noodles or 450 g/1 lb dried *udon*
1.4 L/2½ pt Japanese Broth (see page 24)

topping

4 sheets deep-fried bean curd, halved
200 ml/7 fl oz Premier Japanese Stock (see page 23)
2 Tbsp caster sugar
2½ Tbsp Japanese soy sauce
225 g/8 oz fresh spinach, roughly chopped
2 spring onions, chopped
Seven-spice seasoning (optional)

▶ Rinse the bean curd in hot water to remove excess oil, then place in a pan with the Premier Japanese Stock, sugar and soy sauce. The liquid should just cover the bean curd sheets. Simmer for 20 minutes or until the liquid has reduced by two-thirds.
▶ Bring water to the boil and cook the noodles for 3 minutes. Drain and rinse with cold water then drain again. Divide the noodles among four bowls.
▶ Blanch the spinach in boiling water for 1 minute, then drain and squeeze out the excess water.
▶ Heat the Japanese Broth.
▶ Top the noodles with two pieces of bean curd, spinach and spring onions.
▶ Pour over the Japanese Broth and sprinkle with the seven spice-seasoning.

Japanese Hot Pot Noodles

Japanese Hot Pot Noodles (*Nabeyaki Udon*) are usually based on a soy sauce flavoured Japanese broth, so the *miso* used here makes a change. Make this a vegetable-only meal by omitting the chicken and using cubes of bean curd rolled in flour and shallow-fried. If you use dried noodles, boil them until they are almost cooked.

1.8 L/3¼ pt Premier Japanese Stock (see page 23)
225 g/8 oz boneless, skinless chicken breast, diced
75 g/3 oz sliced carrots
75 g/3 oz chopped turnip
½ leek, sliced diagonally
2 Tbsp Japanese rice wine
8 fresh *shiitake* mushrooms
600 g/1¼ lb parboiled, fresh *udon* noodles, rinsed, or 450 g/1 lb dried *udon*
8 Tbsp *miso* paste

▶ Put the stock, chicken, carrots, turnips and leek in a pan, bring to the boil then add the rice wine and mushrooms. Simmer for 10 to 12 minutes.

▶ Add the noodles to the pan and cook for 3 minutes (adding the noodles will cool the mixture). Stir in the *miso* paste. Continue to heat and when the liquid comes back to the boil, the hot pot is ready to serve.

Seafood and Vegetables with Noodles

Kishimen are broad, flat noodles that resemble Italian fettucine. Crab sticks can be bought from specialist food shops.

8 mange touts, trimmed
600 g/1¼ lb parboiled fresh *kishimen* or *udon* noodles, or 450 g/1 lb dried *udon*
8 crab sticks
½ sheet seaweed paper, cut into four strips
4 spring onions, chopped
1.4 L/2½ pt Japanese Broth (see page 24)

▶ Cook the mange touts in boiling water for 2 minutes. Rinse with cold water and set aside.
▶ Bring water to the boil and cook the noodles for 3 minutes. Rinse under cold water, then drain. Divide the noodles among four bowls.
▶ Divide the mange touts, crab sticks, seaweed and spring onions among four bowls. Heat the broth and pour into the bowls. Serve immediately.

Chilled Noodle Soup

A cold soup that is a generous meal for two, or a palate-refreshing starter for four. A regular pear is an acceptable substitute for an Asian pear.

225 g/8 oz *soba* noodles
1 tsp sesame oil
1.1 L/2 pt Chicken Stock (see page 22)
5-centimetre/2-inch piece white radish, cut into matchsticks
225 ml/8 fl oz cooking liquid from white radish
½ cucumber, thinly sliced
Salt
1½ tsp rice vinegar
Pinch granulated sugar
Pinch cayenne pepper mixed with paprika
2 hard-boiled eggs, thinly sliced
½ Asian pear, peeled, cored and thinly sliced

▶ Cook the noodles following the instructions on the packet, then drain and rinse under cold water. Drain, again place into a bowl, and toss with the sesame oil and 125 ml/4 fl oz of the stock.
▶ Cook the white radish in a pan of boiling water for 10 minutes or until tender. Add 225 ml/8 fl oz of the water used to cook the radish to the remaining 1 L/1¾ pt of stock.
▶ Put the cucumber in a colander and toss with salt. Leave for 1 hour, then rinse and drain before drying on kitchen paper. Place in a bowl and mix in the vinegar, sugar, cayenne and paprika.
▶ Divide the noodles among four bowls, and pour over one-quarter of the remaining stock. Arrange the slices of egg, cucumber and pear on top.

Japanese Marinated Chicken with Noodles (*Tori-nanban*)

This dish really only comes into it own if the chicken is marinated for at least 15 minutes. This gives the chicken – or indeed a bean curd substitute if preferred – a chance to extract the flavour from the sauce.

3 boneless, skinless chicken breasts, sliced diagonally into bite-sized pieces
2 Tbsp Japanese soy sauce
1 leek, thinly sliced diagonally
1.4 L/2½ pt Japanese Broth (see page 24)
400 g/14 oz dried *soba* noodles
Radish sprouts or watercress, to garnish
Seven-spice seasoning (optional)

▶ Marinate the chicken in soy sauce for at least 15 minutes. Put the chicken, leek and broth in a pan and bring to the boil, then simmer for 10 to 15 minutes or until the chicken is cooked. Occasionally, skim scum off the surface.

▶ Meanwhile, bring a large saucepan of water to the boil. Add the noodles and cook for 5 to 6 minutes. Drain and rinse under cold water. Drain again, then divide the noodles among four bowls.

▶ Spoon chicken, leek and broth over the noodles. Sprinkle over the radish sprouts or watercress and seven-spice powder. Serve immediately.

Classic Japanese Cold Noodles

To eat this dish, place some of the garnish into your Dipping Broth, then taking some noodles from the communal plate with your chopsticks, dip them into the broth and enjoy!

450 g/1 lb *somen* noodles
700 ml/1¼ pt Dipping Broth (see page 24), chilled

garnish
1 sheet seaweed paper, cut into fine strips
3 spring onions, chopped
2 tsp Japanese horseradish
8 basil leaves, shredded
Ice cubes

▶ Bring a large pan of water to the boil and add the noodles. When the water returns to the boil, pour in a small cupful of cold water to reduce the temperature. When the water comes back to the boil, remove the noodles immediately. Drain and rinse under cold water, then drain again.
▶ Place the ice cubes on a large serving plate and top with the noodles. Pour the chilled broth into four small bowls, and serve the garnishes separately.

Fermented Soy beans with Noodles

This is a modern combination of two traditional Japanese ingredients – *natto* and *udon*. While fermented soy beans (*natto*) are not to everyone's taste, but they are a rich source of nutritious protein. They are available in specialist food shops.

6 okra
Salt
200 g/7 oz fermented soy beans
1 Tbsp bonito flakes
1 spring onion, chopped
1 tsp English mustard
400 g/4 tsp Japanese soy sauce
400 g/14 oz parboiled, fresh *udon* noodles, or 450 g/1 lb dried *udon*
500 ml/1 pt Dipping Broth (see page 24), chilled
½ sheet seaweed paper, finely cut

▶ Sprinkle the okra with salt, and roll them backwards and forwards on a chopping board to remove the hairs. Blanch in boiling water for 1 minute, then drain and chop into small pieces.

▶ Mix the okra, soy beans, bonito flakes, spring onion, mustard and soy sauce together in a bowl.

▶ Bring a saucepan of water to the boil and add the noodles. Cook for 3 minutes, then rinse and drain. Divide the noodles among four bowls.

▶ Pile the okra and soy bean mixture onto the noodles. Pour over the chilled broth and sprinkle with seaweed. Serve immediately.

Mushrooms with Chilled Noodles

This is a modern Japanese summer dish. Easily digested, it can be served as a first course or as a light, refreshing lunch. Tinned button mushrooms can be substituted for the *nameko* mushrooms.

400 g/14 oz dried *soba* noodles
400 g/14 oz tinned *nameko* or tinned button mushrooms
325 g/11 oz white radish, peeled and cut into fine strips
½ sheet seaweed paper, cut into fine strips
500 ml/1 pt Dipping Broth (see page 24), chilled

▶ Bring a large saucepan of water to the boil and cook the noodles for 5 to 6 minutes or according to the instructions on the packet. Rinse under cold water and drain well. Divide the noodles among four bowls.

▶ Mix the mushrooms and white radish together in a bowl, then pile them onto the noodles. Sprinkle with seaweed and pour over the chilled broth immediately before serving.

Chicken and Soured Plum Noodles

This recipe uses traditional Japanese ingredients to create a contemporary dish. The bite of the soured plums in the Dipping Broth gives extra zest to the cold noodles.

3 boneless, skinless chicken breasts
12 okra
Salt
400 g/14 oz dried *soba* noodles
4 large sour plums, stoned and finely chopped
500 ml/1 pt Dipping Broth (see page 24)
4 spring onions, sliced

▶ In a pan, bring water to the boil and cook the chicken until cooked through. Remove and leave to cool. Tear the chicken into small strips.
▶ Sprinkle the okra with salt and roll them backwards and forwards on a chopping board to remove the hairs. Blanch in boiling water for 1 minute, then drain and cut into 1-centimetre/ ½-inch slices.
▶ Put the soured plums into a mortar with a little broth, and grind into a thin paste. In a bowl, combine the paste with the remaining broth, and refrigerate.
▶ Bring a large saucepan of water to the boil and cook the noodles for 5 to 6 minutes. Drain and rinse under cold water. Drain again, then divide the noodles among four bowls.
▶ Top the noodles with the chicken and okra, and pour over the soured plum sauce. Garnish with the sliced spring onions and serve immediately.

Japanese Seafood Noodle Stir-Fry (Yaki Udon)

Stir-frying coaxes maximum flavour out of seafood ingredients and gives the noodles a smooth, slippery texture.

400 g/14 oz dried *udon* noodles
2 Tbsp sunflower oil
175 g/6 oz squid, cleaned and sliced
450 g/1 lb large cooked prawns, shelled and deveined
4 spring onions, roughly chopped
225 g/8 oz bean sprouts
15 fresh *shiitake* mushrooms, sliced
4 tsp dried green seaweed, soaked in hot water and drained
4 Tbsp bonito flakes
4 Tbsp Japanese or light soy sauce
Salt and freshly ground black pepper

▶ Bring water to the boil, add the noodles and cook for 7 to 15 minutes. Rinse under cold water and drain.
▶ Heat the oil in a wok or frying pan until very hot and stir-fry the squid and prawns for 2 minutes. Add the spring onions, bean sprouts, mushrooms and seaweed and stir-fry for 2 minutes.
▶ Add the noodles and remaining ingredients and seasonings, and stir-fry for 1 minute. Divide the noodles and seafood among four plates and serve.

Shredded White Radish with Noodles

This is an original take on a classic Japanese dish. The Japanese would use white radish (*daikon*) sprouts (the greenery from the top of the radish root) rather than radish sprouts or watercress, so try to get some *daikon* from a Japanese food shop.

400 g/14 oz dried *soba* noodles
325 g/11 oz white radish, peeled and cut into fine strips
Radish sprouts or watercress, rinsed
1 sheet seaweed paper, cut into fine strips
700 ml/1¼ pt Dipping Broth (see page 24)
2 spring onions, chopped
2.5-centimetre/1 inch piece root ginger, shredded and ground

▶ In a pan, bring a quantity of water to the boil, and cook the noodles for 3 to 6 minutes. Rinse and cool under cold water, and drain.

▶ Mix the noodles, white radish, and radish sprouts or watercress together in a bowl. Divide the mixture among four bowls and sprinkle over with seaweed.

▶ Serve the chilled broth, spring onions, and ginger separately.

Deep-fried Vegetables and Noodles (Ten Zaru)

One of the most famous dishes in Japanese cuisine, *tempura* needs little introduction. Both the *tempura* and the noodles should be dipped into the broth as they are eaten.

Vegetable oil for deep-frying

batter

1 egg, beaten
9 Tbsp plain flour
250 ml/9 fl oz cold water
1 medium aubergine, halved and sliced
4 fresh *shiitake* mushrooms, stalks removed
125 g/4 oz carrots, cut into matchsticks
16 green beans, trimmed
400 g/14 oz dried *soba* noodles
700 ml/1¼ pt Dipping Broth (see page 24), chilled

▶ Fill a pan one-third full of oil and heat to 350°F/175°C. Check the temperature by dropping in some batter or a piece of bread; if it bubbles and floats to the surface, the oil is at the right temperature.

▶ To make the batter, mix the egg, flour and water lightly in a bowl. The batter should be quite lumpy with some flour visible on top of the mixture.

▶ Dip the aubergine and mushrooms in the batter and deep-fry until golden brown. Dip the carrots and green beans in the batter in small bundles and deep-fry. Place all vegetables on kitchen paper to drain.

▶ Bring a large saucepan of water to the boil and cook the noodles for 4 to 6 minutes, or according to the instructions on the packet. Rinse under cold water and drain well.

▶ Divide the noodles among four plates, and place the vegetables on a serving plate. Pour the chilled broth into four small bowls and serve.

Stir-fry and Curry Sauce

Curry sauce is a new topping for noodles in Japan, although there is a precedent for this hot dish – a spicy noodle curry soup. The popularity of this soup attests to the modern appeal of the noodles and curry combination.

600 g/1¼ lb parboiled, *udon* noodles
3 Tbsp sunflower oil
1 clove garlic, crushed
1 medium onion, sliced
1 small red pepper, sliced
1 aubergine, quartered lengthwise and sliced into 5-centimetre/2-inch wedges
300 g/10 oz sliced button mushrooms

sauce

2 Tbsp hot water
½ vegetable or chicken stock cube, crumbled
4 Tbsp tomato ketchup
1 to 2 tsp hot curry powder
½ tsp salt
Coriander leaves

▶ Bring a large saucepan of water to the boil, add the fresh noodles and cook for 3 minutes. Rinse under cold water and drain.

▶ Heat the oil in a wok or frying pan until very hot and stir-fry the garlic and onion for 1 minute. Add the pepper, aubergine and mushrooms and stir-fry for 4 to 5 minutes or until the aubergine has softened.

▶ Mix the sauce ingredients, except the coriander, together in a bowl. Add the noodles and sauce to the vegetables and stir-fry for 1 to 2 minutes. Sprinkle with coriander and serve immediately.

Miso Noodles with Beef and Vegetables

The sauce in this modern Japanese stir-fried dish is based on *miso* (a Japanese soy product). There are two types of *miso* – red and white. The red is more strongly flavoured and saltier than the white.

400 g/14 oz dried *udon* noodles
200 g/7 oz green cabbage
150 g/5 oz green beans
2 Tbsp sunflower oil
225 g/8 oz rump steak, sliced diagonally into bite-sized pieces
1 small red pepper, chopped into bite-sized pieces
10 fresh *shiitake* mushrooms, quartered
Pinch of salt and chilli powder
2 Tbsp red *miso* paste
2 Tbsp Japanese or light soy sauce
2 Tbsp sweet rice wine
1 spring onion, chopped

▶ Bring a large saucepan of water to the boil, add the noodles and cook for 7 to 15 minutes, depending on the instructions on the packet. Rinse under cold water and drain.

▶ Blanch the cabbage and beans for 2 minutes in boiling water. Refresh under cold water. Cut the cabbage into bite-sized pieces and halve the beans.

▶ Heat the oil in a wok or frying pan until very hot, and fry the beef for 2 minutes. Add the cabbage, beans and mushrooms and sprinkle on salt and chilli powder. Stir-fry for 2 to 3 minutes.

▶ Mix the *miso*, soy sauce and rice wine together in a bowl. Add the noodles and *miso* mixture to the wok and stir-fry for 1 minute. Divide the noodles among four plates and sprinkle over the spring onions. Serve immediately.

Classic Japanese Noodles with Five Toppings (Okame Udon)

A substantial soup-cum-meal that is perfect for a late supper.

600 g/1¼ lb parboiled, fresh *udon* noodles or 450 g/1 lb dried *udon*
1.4 L/2½ pt Japanese Broth (see page 24)

topping

4 fresh *shiitake* mushrooms, stalks removed
350 ml/12 fl oz Premier Japanese Stock (see page 23)
2½ Tbsp Japanese soy sauce
2½ Tbsp sweet rice wine
225 g/8 oz fresh spinach leaves
4 slices Japanese fish cake or 4 crab sticks
Radish sprouts or watercress

egg pancake

2 eggs
2 tsp sweet rice wine
¼ tsp soy sauce
Pinch of salt
2 tsp vegetable oil

▶ To make the topping – In a large pan, bring the mushrooms, stock, soy sauce and rice wine to the boil and simmer for 8 to 10 minutes. Set aside to allow the mushrooms to soften (see page 19).

▶ To make the pancake – Beat the eggs, rice wine, soy sauce and salt in a bowl. Heat a little of the oil in a non-stick frying pan and pour in one-third of the egg mixture to cover evenly. When it is half set, roll it up on one side. Add a little more oil (if necessary) and pour in half of the remaining egg mixture. Leave to half-set, then roll the egg pancake to the other side of the frying pan, picking up the just-set pancake. Add more oil and the remaining egg mixture, and repeat the process. Leave to cool, then cut into four pieces.

▶ Cook the spinach in boiling water for 1 to 2 minutes. Drain then rinse with cold water, squeezing to remove excess liquid. Divide into four portions.

▶ In a large pan, bring water to the boil and cook the noodles for 3 minutes. Rinse, drain, and divide among four bowls.

▶ Heat the Japanese Broth. Meanwhile, discard the liquid from the mushrooms, and top the noodles with equal servings of mushroom, pancake, spinach and fish cake or crab sticks. Scatter over the radish sprouts or watercress. Pour over the hot broth, and serve immediately.

bean thread noodles

chapter 4

Light Prawn and Noodle Soup (Pho Tôm)

This is a very light and delicious soup. To make it a little more substantial, prawn balls can be added. Ready-made prawn or fish balls are sold in vacuum-packed plastic bags in Chinese food shops.

850 ml/1½ pt Vegetable Stock (see page 23)
8 button mushrooms, sliced
2 cucumbers, peeled and cut into matchsticks
175 g/6 oz bean thread vermicelli noodles
225 g/8 oz fresh prawns, cooked and shelled
4 large cooked prawn, shells intact
⅔ cup fish sauce

▶ Pour the stock into a pan and add the mushrooms. Set aside.

▶ Arrange the cucumbers and prawns on serving plates. Soak the noodles in boiled water, slightly cooled, for 5 minutes. Drain and divide between four bowls. Meanwhile, bring the stock and mushrooms to the boil and then simmer, adding the prawn balls (see below).

▶ To eat – top the noodles with cucumber and prawns, and pour over the hot stock. Spoon in fish sauce for taste and garnish with an unshelled prawn.

prawn balls

175 g/6 oz cooked prawns, shelled and deveined, and mashed
1 small hard-boiled egg, mashed
1 small onion, very finely chopped
1 egg, beaten
Salt and pepper

▶ Mix the ingredients together in a bowl with your hands. Shape the mixture into small balls, and drop into a simmering broth or stock for 5 minutes to cook.

Stir-fried Bean Sprouts and Noodles

Other than allowing time to soak and drain the noodles, this light and tasty meal can be prepared in minutes. The secret lies in having everything ready and to hand.

1 Tbsp vegetable oil
2 small onions, thinly sliced
4 cloves garlic, chopped
75 g/3 oz bean sprouts
1 red pepper, thinly sliced
175 g/6 oz bean thread noodles, soaked in hot water for 10 minutes,drained, and cut into 8-centimetre/3-inch lengths
125 ml/4 fl oz Chicken Stock (see page 22)
1 Tbsp fish sauce
2 spring onions, thinly sliced
1 Tbsp chopped coriander
Freshly ground black pepper

▶ Heat the oil in a wok over a high heat and add the onions and garlic. Sauté for 2 minutes or until the edges begin to brown.

▶ Add the bean sprouts and red pepper and stir-fry for 30 seconds, then the noodles and stir-fry for 1 minute. Stir in the Chicken Stock and fish sauce, and toss to combine. Add the spring onions and remove from heat. Serve sprinkled with the coriander and black pepper.

Vietnamese Vegetarian Spring Rolls
(Bánh Cuôn Chay Viêt Nam)

It is important to use ingredients that will not break through the delicate rice paper – the ingredients must be minced or finely chopped.

MAKES 8 ROLLS

dipping sauce

150 ml/5 fl oz fish sauce
1 clove garlic, finely chopped
1 red chilli, finely chopped
2 tsp lemon or lime juice
1 tsp cider vinegar
1 tsp granulated sugar
50 g/2 oz finely chopped, salted peanuts (optional)

spring rolls

50 g/2 oz bean thread vermicelli noodles
12 dried *shiitake* mushrooms
3 dried wood ear fungus
200-g/7-oz tin water chestnuts, drained and chopped
2 cloves garlic, crushed
1 carrot, cut into fine strips
1 onion, cut into fine strips
2 Tbsp chopped coriander
2 spring onions, sliced
1 Tbsp fish sauce
Freshly ground black pepper
1 egg, beaten
8 sheets round *banh trang* rice paper, measuring 20 centimetres/8 inches across
Vegetable oil for shallow-frying

to serve

1 Webb lettuce
Sprigs of fresh coriander and mint
½ cucumber, peeled and cut into matchstick strips

▶ Combine the dipping sauce ingredients and stir well.

▶ Soak the noodles in boiled water until soft. Drain thoroughly, then cut into shorter strands with kitchen scissors.

▶ Soak the mushrooms and wood ear fungus in hot, previously boiled water, until soft. Drain and gently squeeze out excess water, then finely chop.

▶ Place the noodles, mushroom, wood ear fungus, water chestnuts, garlic, carrot, onion, coriander, spring onion, fish sauce, black pepper and egg in a large mixing bowl. Mix and knead the mixture by hand until it is stiff enough to be shaped.

▶ Pour boiled water, slightly cooled, into a large bowl. Spread a clean teatowel on your work surface. Dip a rice paper into the water, and place it on the teatowel. The rice paper will become soft and pliable.

▶ Place a small amount of the noodle mixture in the middle of the rice paper, and form into a sausage shape. Fold the bottom edge over the mixture, tucking it under the mixture. Fold the left and right edges over to the middle. Roll the parcel away from you to seal in the mixture. Repeat until all the mixture is used.

▶ Heat the vegetable oil until hot in a large frying pan. Shallow-fry the rolls a few at a time, turning frequently until the mixture is cooked and the rice paper golden. Drain on kitchen paper.

▶ To serve, place each roll on a lettuce leaf with a little mint, coriander and cucumber. To eat, fold a lettuce leaf around the roll and dip into the sauce.

Fried Noodles with Spicy Bean Curd

With some types of bean curd, it is best to drain and squeeze out excess water before dicing. To squeeze the bean curd without risk of it crumbling, lay it between two flat plates and press gently.

225 g/8 oz bean thread noodles
4 Tbsp vegetable oil
300 g/10 oz bean curd, diced
3 cloves garlic, crushed
4 shallots, finely chopped
200 g/7 oz bean sprouts
400 g/14 oz frozen green beans, halved
2 spring onions, chopped
2 Tbsp roasted peanuts, crushed
2 Tbsp dried prawns, chopped
3 to 5 small green chillies, chopped
2½ Tbsp granulated brown sugar
6 Tbsp fish sauce
125 ml/4 fl oz fresh lemon juice

garnish

2 Tbsp crisply fried onion
Fresh coriander
1 medium red chilli, sliced
4 lime wedges

▶ Soak the noodles in boiling water for 5 minutes. Rinse under cold water and drain.

▶ Heat half the oil in a wok or frying pan, and fry the bean curd until golden brown. Drain on kitchen paper.

▶ Add the remaining oil to the wok, and fry the garlic and shallots for 30 seconds. Stir in the bean sprouts, beans and spring onions. Add the noodles, bean curd, peanuts, dried prawns and chilli. Stir to mix well, before seasoning with the sugar, fish sauce and lemon juice. Stir thoroughly.

▶ Divide the noodles among four plates, and top with the garnish. Serve immediately.

Thai Casseroled Prawns and Noodles *(Kung Op Woon Sen)*

The size of the prawns is unimportant, and lobster tails or crab claws can be substituted. But for maximum flavour, use fresh, not frozen produce. This recipe makes four generous servings.

soup stock

450 ml/16 fl oz Chicken Stock (see page 22)
2 Tbsp oyster sauce
1½ Tbsp Chinese dark soy sauce
½ Tbsp sesame oil
½ tsp granulated sugar

prawns and noodles

2 bacon rashers, cut into 2.5-centimetre/1-inch pieces
20 large fresh prawns, shelled and deveined
1 bunch coriander, rinsed and chopped
25 g/1 oz root ginger, finely chopped
1 clove garlic, chopped
1 tsp white peppercorns, crushed
225 g/8 oz bean thread noodles, soaked in hot water for 5 minutes
1 tsp butter
2 Tbsp Chinese dark soy sauce
2 Tbsp roughly chopped coriander leaves and stems

▶ Place the soup stock ingredients in a pan and bring to the boil. Simmer for 5 minutes, then set aside to cool.

▶ In a heatproof casserole or heavy saucepan, lay the bacon to cover the base. Top with the prawns, coriander, root ginger, garlic and peppercorns. Cover with noodles, then add the butter, soy sauce and soup stock.

▶ Place on the heat, cover and bring to the boil. Simmer for 5 minutes, mix well, and sprinkle over with the coriander. Cover and cook for 5 minutes, or until the prawns are cooked through. Remove excess soup stock before serving.

Spicy Noodle Salad with Prawns (Yam Woonsen)

This is a hot Thai salad, and the fish sauce is an essential flavour-enhancing ingredient. Prepare the dish at least 30 minutes before serving so the full sweet, hot flavour has time to mature.

200 g/7 oz bean thread noodles
16 large fresh prawns, shelled and deveined
1 tsp fish sauce
2 tsp freshly squeezed lemon juice
1 tsp granulated brown sugar
1 Tbsp sunflower oil
1 small red pepper, finely chopped
2 sticks celery, thinly sliced
125 g/4 oz carrots, cut into matchsticks
2 spring onions, chopped
4 iceberg lettuce leaves
Coriander leaves

dressing

2 shallots, finely chopped
1 dry red chilli, crushed
3 small green chillis, chopped
4 Tbsp fish sauce
125 ml/4 fl oz fresh lemon juice
4½ Tbsp granulated brown sugar
1 Tbsp sunflower oil

▶ Soak the noodles in warm water for 5 minutes or according to the instructions on the packet. Rinse under cold water and drain.
▶ Marinate the prawns in the fish sauce, lemon juice and sugar for 5 minutes. Meanwhile, mix together the dressing ingredients in a bowl.
▶ Heat 1 tablespoon of oil in a frying pan and stir-fry the prawns until cooked.
▶ Put the peppers, celery, carrot, spring onions and noodles in a bowl and mix together. Place a lettuce leaf on each plate and spoon in the noodle mixture. Top with prawns and sprinkle with coriander to serve.

Korean Cellophane Noodles with Mixed Vegetables (Chapchae)

This is a colourful, vegetable-packed noodle dish with a multitude of different textures. Once the vegetables have been prepared, it is very quick to assemble and cook.

- **6 dried wood ear fungus, soaked in hot water for 30 minutes**
- **150 g/5 oz young, fresh spinach leaves**
- **2 Chinese leaves**
- **3 fresh *shiitake* or oyster mushrooms, thinly sliced**
- **4 spring onions, thickly sliced diagonally**
- **1 small courgette, cut into fine strips**
- **1 carrot, cut into fine strips**
- **3 Tbsp vegetable oil**
- **1 Tbsp sesame oil**
- **3 cloves garlic, crushed, finely chopped**
- **2 small fresh red chillies, seeded and cut into fine strips**
- **200 g/7 oz bean thread noodles, soaked in hot water for 5 minutes and drained**
- **1 Tbsp Japanese soy sauce**
- **1 tsp granulated sugar**
- **Salt**

▶ Drain the wood ear fungus, and cut out the stems. Thinly sliced.

▶ Add the spinach to a pan of boiling water. Cover and boil for 2 minutes, then drain and rinse under cold water. Drain and squeeze out excess water. Separate the leaves.

▶ Discard the curly outer part of the Chinese leaves. Cut the V-shaped core of the leaves into fine strips. Combine the spinach, wood ear fungus and *shiitake* mushrooms, spring onions, courgettes, carrot and Chinese leaves.

▶ Heat the oils in a deep skillet. Add the garlic and chile, and stir-fry for 10 seconds. Add the mixed vegetables and stir-fry for 3 to 4 minutes until the vegetables are tender, but crisp. Turn the heat to low and stir in the noodles, soy sauce, sugar and salt. Cook for 2 minutes and serve immediately.